4ᵗʰ & Hell

This is the first in a series about the reality of a certain group of athletes—football players. The series is based on a true story that chronicles the life-lessons learned from coaching a Canadian football team, the Niagara X-Men, as they try to compete in the United States. It's a reality show in writing.

The Niagara X-Men exist to give student-athletes a second chance, a chance to advance to university. The X-Men organization provides the stage on which deserving student-athletes have the opportunity to practice their skills and compete, in the hopes of moving to the next level.

The Niagara X-Men are a non-profit organization operating in southern Ontario. They receive no public or outside funding.

Head coach Gino Arcaro welcomes questions and comments. Please email him at: gino@ginoarcaro.com.

4ᵗʰ & Hell
Season 1

Author: Gino Arcaro
Website: www.ginoarcaro.com
email: gino@ginoarcaro.com

Jordan Publications Inc.
Canada

Cover Art: Leon "Eklipz" Robinson
Editor: Janice Arcaro
Assisting Editor: Matthew Dawson
Design: Jessica Ingram
Design: Shelley Palomba
Design Consultant: Luciana Millone
Logistics Manager: Jordan Mammoliti
Technical Support: Leeann King

Arcaro, Gino, 1957
ISBN 978-1927851036
http://www.ginoarcaro.com
Printed in Canada

Gino Arcaro's Story

I started lifting as a dysfunctional 12-year-old, trying to overcome my obesity. Lifting transformed my life physically and mentally. I have been lifting for over 43 consecutive years, 100% natural. I lift almost every day. It's part of who I am and it will always be, but it doesn't define me.

At 18, I started my policing career. A few years later, I became a SWAT team officer and then at the age of 26, a detective. At the same age, I accepted the head coach position at a high school, a decision that began a lengthy volunteer coaching career. I wrote my SWAT No-Huddle Offense and Defense manuals, (and recently published them) explaining the systems I had created and refined throughout 40 seasons of coaching football at the high school, college and semi-pro levels.

After 15 years, I left policing to teach law enforcement at the local college. During the next 20 years, I became a bestselling academic author, writing 6 law enforcement textbooks that are used in colleges throughout Ontario. Also during that time, I earned a Master degree, an undergraduate degree, and Level 3 NCCP Coaching certification. Then, in 2001, I opened a 24-hour gym called X Fitness Welland Inc. The gym continues to enjoy success in its second decade of operations. *eXplode: The X Fitness Training System* is a book I wrote that explains my workout system, based on 40+ years of lifting.

In 2010, I left teaching to make the literary transition to motivational writer. My first book, *Soul of a Lifter* was published in 2011. Since then, I've added several books. *Blunt Talk* is the name of a series I'm writing dealing with everything from fat loss to interrogation. *Soul of an Entrepreneur* is another series written to enlighten business owners – current and potential. In the series, *4th and Hell,* I tell "David vs Goliath" tales about my Canadian club football team playing in the United States. When my first granddaughter was born, I wrote, *Beauty of a Dream* and the following year, I wrote *Mondo piu Bello* to commemorate the birth of her cousin. In 2014 I began my "Happy Kids Books" series with *Be Fit Don't Quit.*

I am motivated in my writing by my belief that we all have a potential soul of a lifter. We are called to lift for life. We can lift ourselves. We can lift others.

Keep lifting,
Gino Arcaro

Prologue

A "friction" book.
It's mostly fact, not fiction,
that caused a ton of friction.

The purpose of the 4th & Hell book series
is to tell true stories, each with a separate,
but connected meaning.

I
Two Miracles

"There are two ways to live: you can live as if nothing is a miracle;
you can live as if everything is a miracle."
- Albert Einstein

Niagara X-Men   36
Buffalo State College   38

00:00
4th quarter

A football scoreboard is like a communications director. It sends a simple message for the benefit of the decision-makers reading it. Nothing complex. Simple. Efficient. To the point. Easy to process.

The teams. The score. What quarter. Time remaining. Down and distance.

At first glance, this scoreboard showed:

1. The winner and the loser. Somewhere deep in the recesses of our minds, we have been conditioned to classify those who score more points as winners and those who score less, losers. A Pavlovian response to counting numbers and then defining success by how they add up.
2. The game was close. Only two points separated the two teams. Must have been exciting and entertaining!
3. Time ran out. 4th quarter + four zeros on the clock usually means time's up. You've had your chance. It's over — no second chance. You have to live with what happened.

The scoreboard is supposed to be a benefit to a football coach. It's supposed to help him make warp-speed informed decisions. Nothing intricate. Nothing complicated.

But sometimes, a football scoreboard can be a distraction.

First, a scoreboard doesn't tell the whole story. Not even close. It's only a snapshot of what's really happening. A synopsis. A general narrative or quick summary. But not the whole story. Second, the information may be so shocking that the human mind simply cannot process it. Crosses up the wires.

This was one of those times. The information made no sense. It was severe. It was distracting. It was… shocking. Shocking enough to distort rational thinking.

This scoreboard did not say:

1. The visiting team was from Canada. The home team was American.
2. There was absolutely no possible way that the Canadian team should be that close to beating an American team. This was the Canadian team's first year playing in the United States.
3. Even though the time showed 4 zeros, the game was not finished. The Canadian team had marched 91 yards down the field in less than two minutes to score a touchdown, just as the clock wound down to 4 zeros.
4. One play remained. One last chance for the Canadian team. Time's up, with one last shot at redemption. And, if the Canadian team was successful on this last play, the game would be tied. Overtime!

"Four zeros on the clock" and "fourth quarter" are deeply entrenched in the football coaching vernacular. Players hear it spoken often and emphatically.

"FOURTH QUARTER! DO… NOT… QUIT UNTIL YOU SEE FOUR ZEROS ON THE CLOCK!"

Simple, efficient instructions. Don't quit, don't be lazy. Go full out until you cross the finish line. Empty the tank. Then you can stop. Then you can relax.

Generally, 4 zeros is the finish line. It means "time ran out." Last one out turns off the lights. But with one exception — if a team scores a touchdown on the last play. Then, the finish line gets pushed back. One more play is allowed. A new "last play" happens. It's called a "conversion." A chance to add one or two extra points to the six that were earned by the touchdown. It ain't over til the fat lady sings and she has to do an encore. Turn the lights back on.

A conversion is the rule-makers way of dishing out a bonus.

"You just scored six points? Well, you get a bonus... one more play. Even though time ran out. Seems like the fair thing to do. You can get one or two more points. Your choice coach. One- or two-point bonus."

The problem is that the bonus is not automatic. Not guaranteed. It has to be earned. Not like in the real world.

"Good news, Orville, your sales were up this month. You get a bonus."
"Great."
"Bad news. You have to work for it."
"But, you said the month was over... and it's a bonus."
"Well, it is a bonus... and the month is over... technically speaking, but... just get back to work, will ya? It's time to work for your bonus."

∞

Four zeros and one play left — the time paradox. The curtain falls — momentarily — but the drama continues. THE END... temporarily. The show is over but there's one more scene. Lift the curtain. One more play meant a "call" had to be made. A "call" is football jargon for "rapid decision." Call sounds much cooler than rapid decision.

Football is a time-sensitive and time-restricted game. It penalizes procrastinators. Decisions have to be made within an allotted time, governed by a clock: the 40/25 clock. In some cases, 40 seconds are allowed to make a call. In others, 25. That's it. If time runs out, the ref blows a whistle, throws a yellow flag in the procrastinator's direction, and tells the entire stadium that the coach is incapable of making a decision.

"TWEEEET! Delay of game. That guy over there can't make a decision. 15 yards!"

A 40-second time clock ticking away, screaming,

"We're waiting! 39, 38, 37..."

And, the football legislators don't care how big the decision is. The 40-second clock just keeps ticking.

Workplaces should operate so efficiently.

"What about my proposal? Any idea when I'll get an answer?"
"Well, you know, let me see. I have to call a few people who have to call a few more people who might..."
"TWEEEET... Passing the buck... Demotion."

In this game, the "call" actually needed a total of three decisions. First, whether to try for one point or two. Second, what type of play — pass or run. Third, what specific play.

Down by two points with one play remaining made the first decision a no-brainer. Must go for two — no choice. Some decisions are not decisions at all. They are made for you. You need two points so you try for two points.

The only real question was, how — pass or run? And what kind exactly?

Thousands of calls are made during a coaching career but this one was different. The right call would have serious consequences. The right call would disturb the laws of football — of nature itself. The right call would mean that a Canadian football team would tie an American football team. This would upset the natural order of the football universe.

"You meant hockey, right? A Canadian hockey team would tie an American hockey team."
"No. Football."

The right call would cause shock. Extreme shock. It would send the game into overtime — unless shock waves suspended the game.

"Breaking news! Canadian-American football game suspended due to shock. Film at 11."
"You meant darkness. Suspended due to darkness."
"No. Suspended due to shock."

The shock of a tie game would definitely bring on darkness — but a different kind. A cultural darkness. Darkness brought on by severe depression.

The wrong call, on the other hand, would end the game at 38-36. For them. The wrong call would drop the curtain for good. THE END for real. Roll the credits. Turn off the lights and lock up for good this time. Drive home safely.

The wrong call would mean days and weeks of sympathy.

"You guys came soooo close... only two points."
"Nothing to be ashamed of. You can hold your heads high."
"There's always next year."
"You sure had them scared."
"At least no one died."

Disingenuous sympathy.

Real sympathy is hard to find. It's actually found only in the dictionary — between shit and syphilis.

Either way, right call or wrong call, the Vatican would be notified after the game to report at least one, maybe two, miracles.

Where's my crackberry? Let's see... address book...

Compose email...
  To: Vatican@hotmail.com
  Subject: Miracle(s)

A "miracle" is defined as an extraordinary event, produced by God, that goes beyond the laws of nature. It's an improbability explained only by Divine intervention. One miracle earns beatification. Two verified miracles gets you canonization — full sainthood. Although the Vatican is tough on what constitutes a miracle, I figured this game would be worth a try. A brand new Canadian football team playing against American university players, on the road, in the USA. One play left for the Canadian team to tie and send the game into overtime. The only question was whether the game counted as one or two miracles.

How do you convince the Vatican of two miracles in one football game? Simple. Use an analogy. Drive home final arguments by explaining a hockey analogy. Should work.

"Ok, Texas hockey team plays Canadian hockey team, in Canada..."

Or how about:

"Miami hockey team plays Quebec hockey team, in Laval..."

Expectation? No contest. Annihilation. Ridiculous score. No choice. It has to be. The natural laws of Canadian culture demand it. No red-blooded Canadian team would lose a hockey game to a team from Florida. That would be counter-culture. Canadians would go into shock. Extreme shock.

Does Florida have rinks? Can anyone in Florida skate?

Football is deeply ingrained in American culture. It is stamped in their hearts, flows through their veins, and opens their wallets.

The American financial and emotional investment into football is unrivaled. Their stadiums are shrines, not cow pastures. American weight rooms are state-of-the-art facilities, not dusty dungeons. You don't see rusty 45-pound plates and a 1950s bench in an American university weight room.

Hockey in Canada comes close to this obsession. But, not equal to it. The Canadian total investment in hockey doesn't match the American total investment in football. Total investment – money, mind, heart, and soul. The Canadian hockey passion does not match the Friday Night Lights passion in Odessa, Texas. Close, but not quite.

Canada's Niagara X-Men, in their first season, playing against American university players. This wasn't a simple football game. It was a monumental clash of cultures. David versus Goliath. In pads. In Buffalo. Chicken-wing capital of the world. Just across the border.

"Anything to declare?"
"Slingshot."

∞

In 2005, the Niagara X-Men season started with three games in Canada. Despite an undefeated 3-0 record by a combined score of 117-14, the X-Men were not getting better. In fact, the opposite. They got worse. Regression — attitude and performance. Fat asses. Arrogance. Mistakes. More mistakes. Undefeated but unfulfilled. No opposition. No struggle. No improvement. Going nowhere. Dead-end. Boredom. Regression leads to depression.

The Niagara X-Men — a Goliath-wannabe. A team that thought it was a giant but wasn't. A Goliath-impersonator. A pretend giant. Stronger than the rest by default. Versus David-impersonators — guys with no slingshots.

Not much of a fight. Actually, by definition, not a fight at all. Just a trash-talking, sand-throwing contest. Mud-slinging.

"Ya?"
"Ya."
"Oh ya?
"Yaaaa."

The monotony of "no challenge" is as serious as the anxiety of being "out of your league." Horrific stress. Doing the same thing over and over and over, or, having no clue what to do. Boredom and anxiety. Diametrically opposed stressors, but producers of the same thing. Mind-numbing madness.

The wires start cracking. Fuses break. Meltdown. Slowly at first. It always starts with a slow descent. Then speeds up. An out-of-control downhill race. A wobble leading to a wreck. Correction needed. But you have to stop the downhill slide before you can start the uphill climb. You can't simply change gears from reverse to forward. You have to press down the brake pedal first.

Decision time. Which side of the border? Shrink or stretch? Canada or USA?

Some decisions are no-brainers. You get strong only by competing against the strongest. You have to step out of your comfort zone to get better. You have to amp up the challenge to improve, grow, and reach full potential. How strong your opponent is determines how strong you will become.

True strength is developed through true struggle. If there is no struggle, weakness gets classified as weaker or weakest. It doesn't separate the strong from the weak. There is no Goliath without a David. There is no David without a Goliath. One guy has to be strong and feared. The other guy has to be smaller, weaker, scared, but most of all, must want to get stronger.

Add a slingshot, some balls, a showdown in an alley, and you have a fight.

And someone has to blink. If no one has to blink, it's not a fight. It's not even a disagreement. When no one has to blink, it's a social event.

If you want to get better playing football, the only place to play is in the USA where football is deep-rooted in the culture. Step into the ring where the ring was invented.

So the Niagara X-Men hit the brakes, crossed the border and jumped into the big pool. Straight into the deep end. There was no shallow end. Exclusive cross-border football was the decision. The X-Men became the bridge that helps players cross the border.

American opponents only — NCAA Division III, junior varsity teams. Five games were scheduled in year one. Five USA opponents. All "away" games. All in the USA.

Found an alley. Found a real Goliath — a total of five. All that was needed was a slingshot and some balls.

∞

There is a fine line between empowering and enabling. They are strange relatives. They share the same DNA. They look alike. Sound alike. But the changes they cause are completely opposite. The first is a positive, the second is a negative. Empowering a person fills that person's tank; enabling empties the tank. The enabler and the enabled are both emptied — of hope.

Empowerment is a gift — for the giver and the receiver. Empowerment is an obligation. It is what moves a generation to the next level. Everyone is obliged to put up a ladder for someone else, sometime, or the chain breaks. But, the ladder has to be real and it has to have steps. It should not be too steep and not too flat. It has to be just right. There has to be some climbing involved. Sometimes, there will be falling. Not crashing. Falling. Ladders are a gift. A gift for lost souls. Ladders fuel the soul.

Putting up obstacles instead of ladders is evil. So is seeing a person standing in front of a wall without a ladder and looking away. Turning your back on a person who is ready to climb, but doesn't know how to, blocks that person's potential. It's a crime against nature.

But, enabling is unnatural also. Enabling is a sin — for the giver and the receiver. It is a vicious deception. Enabling promotes a false hope by ignoring the climb.

Ignoring the struggle. Pretending it's not needed. Enabling causes delusion.

There is an even finer line between encouragement and discouragement. Both involve courage. One deposits courage, the other withdraws it.

People can be a source of both encouragement or discouragement. So can attitude — how we perceive a situation. Our worldview determines if an event is a success or a failure and therefore whether we get encouraged or discouraged by it.

∞

Monster. Enter.

You can find anything on the internet. Anything.

Mount Union University. Enter.

"You're from where?"
"Canada."
"And you want to play our junior varsity."
"Yes."
"What's your record?"
"0-0… never played in the USA."

Not born in the USA. Never played in the USA.

"We've got an open date on October 1, 3:00 pm. Need directions?"

Sixty seconds. That was it. That's all it took. No proposals, meetings, interviews. No negotiations. Dial one plus the area code plus the phone number.

Just like when we were kids.

"Can Mount Union come out to play?"
"Just be home before dark."
"Ok. Race you to the park."

The Niagara X-Men's first American game ever — Mount Union University, Alliance, Ohio. The very best NCAA Division III program. A brand-new Canadian team made up of community college players who couldn't get into university, scheduling the New York Yankees of Division III football.

"Main event… David versus the national champions of Goliaths."

Two cultures. Two cultural reactions.

"Oh my."
"They gave us a whupping two years ago."
"Good for you. That's the only way to get better."

Three American coaches. Three mildly shocked responses. But, no trash-talking. No name-calling. Just civility. And… sympathy.

Canadians? Different story.

"HE DID WHAT!?"
"IS HE CRAZY!?"
"DOES HE KNOW WHO THEY ARE!?"

Yes. Mount Union. Winner in 9 of the past 10 NCAA Division III national championships. They don't just win, they destroy.

∞

"Tell the rest of your buses to park over there."

Their equipment manager was simply trying to be helpful when our half-filled school bus arrived at the Mount Union stadium.

"That's it. One bus. We're here."

There is no generic look of shock. Some people squint. Some widen their eyes. The look of shock is a like a signature. It's customized. It can blend with deep sympathy — like the equipment manager's look. He knew what was about to happen.

"Tonight's main event. In the red, white and blue corner, from Gath… the Philistine Warrior… GOLIATH!"

The X-Men got clobbered. Went the distance. 15 rounds. But, a very ugly score. They should have stopped the fight. 35-0 at halftime. 63-0 at the end of the game. Passed for lots of yards though — 122 in the first quarter alone — and kept the score to 7-0. But, instead of impressing their hosts, it just pissed them off. The only consolation was the revelation that a week earlier, a century-old university football program lost to the same Mount Union by a similar score.

The competitive gap was the size of a canyon. The Grand Canyon. But it didn't compare to the gap in physical strength. Goliath was committed to the weight room. Deeply committed. Strength training and football work together just like skating and hockey. American football players don't have a choice about lifting weights. They work out or they don't play. They get it. They understand. American players don't simply show up at the gym when they feel like it and do whatever workout they read about in some bodybuilding magazine. They follow structured workouts, designed and supervised by a real strength coach.

In American university football, the strength coach is probably the most important staff member after the head coach. Why? The weight room tilts the playing field.

We were not on the same strength-training planet, let alone playing field, as our American opponents. Not in commitment. Not in performance. It was obvious that a five-year plan was needed to become competitive. A paradigm shift. A cultural transformation had to happen to inject a different attitude. And, it had to start with strength training.

Every football journey starts with a very small lift. And, a small slingshot.

Goliath   1
David   0

The next three games in the USA weren't much better. Winless — an 0-4 record going into the season finale. Combined score of 212-66. Undefeated in Canada, winless in the USA. All in one season. From Goliath impersonator to David-wannabe.

One game left. Versus Buffalo State College JV. They had a tough, successful Division III football program. They knew our entire offensive system. We knew their skill and strength level. No sign of hope for this game. No way a start-up Canadian team can compete with a Buffalo, New York post-secondary machine.

Buffalo State dressed 83 players. Our 29 car-pooled to the game in mini-vans.

Alley #5. Goliath #5. David was reeling. On the ropes.

∞

Football games are 60-minute events, neatly compartmentalized into four quarters or two halves. The mid-point is "halftime." It lasts fifteen minutes. Fifteen minutes, the entire Buffalo stadium had to stare at the scoreboard in disbelief.

Niagara X-Men   24
Buffalo State College 24

The distraction began. How can anyone be expected to think properly when the scoreboard is announcing a score that made no sense? A tied score could not be explained rationally. Not in the X-Men's first season. Not when the X-Men had never been competitive for even one minute in any of the previous four USA games. Not with 29 players who were overmatched at every position.

∞

There is no rule that says miracles have to occur on separate days. Technically, the halftime score was miracle #1. "38-36" with one play left was miracle #2, regardless of how the game would end. And, if we tied it, a case for miracle #3 would get strong consideration. However, an overtime win would be off the miracle charts; the Vatican would have to waive the five-year waiting period for sainthood.

∞

And then, with 4 zeros on the clock, the referee "spotted" the ball for the final play, the two-point conversion. "Spotted" is a strange football term for putting the ball on the ground so the next play can start. The distance between the spotted ball and the end zone is so close that it makes you wonder why the rule makers gave the offense such an advantage. It's an incredibly short distance to move a ball to get a two-point bonus.

The 40-second clock started counting down. Forty seconds to make a call. Plenty of time to make an intelligent call. Between the time that the referee raised his arms to signal our touchdown and the "spotting" of the ball, there was more than enough time to make what amounted to a no-brainer decision — pass the ball.

Pass the ball with a spread formation, using 5 receivers — the maximum amount of receivers allowed by football law. Easy decision. Pass. Just like we've done for 75% of every game since the early 1990s when we started using a unique warp-speed pass-oriented, no-huddle spread offense. Just like we've done for 75% of every practice. Just like we did for 75% of the final drive that tied this game.

We pass more often than anyone. We never hide it. No trick plays. No secrets. In fact, we actually tell the defense what we will be doing before every play. The defense can hear:

1. That we will be passing.
2. To who.
3. Where on the field the pass will go.

Train like you fight — fight like you train.

What you focus on grows.

Do what you believe in — believe in what you do.

Stick to what you do best.

Passing a lot means you will likely get very good at passing and you should do a lot of it during games. Especially during crucial moments. No-huddle passing gets big yards and big scores. Even if the defense is better than you. Even if you can't move the opponent because he is stronger. Wear them out. Physically and mentally. Tire them out and move them out of your way.

Some decisions are no-brainers.

Pass it on.

∞

II
Three yards

"The distance between insanity and genius is measured only by success."
- Bruce Furstein

"HE'S GOING FOR TWO, WALLY! WHAT A GAMBLE!"
"You're right Barney. If he makes it, he's a genius. But if he doesn't, he'll sure look stupid!!"

Football has a strange scoring system and an even stranger definition of "genius."

Football is the only sport that allows a supplementary scoring attempt — a chance to earn "extra" points after a team scores. Although the six points earned by scoring a touchdown seems fair and generous, the rule-makers didn't think that was enough. So, the team that scored the touchdown gets to try for extra points. The slang term for this play is a "conversion," or "convert." It's worth one or two points depending on how it's scored. Everyone calls it a convert or conversion, except the rulebook, where it's simply called a "try."

The extra-point play requires a decision: try for one point or try for two points. The difference between the two choices is the strategy used. The type of play. If a team takes the easy way and decides to kick the ball through the uprights, the try is valued at one point. To earn two points, the ball must be carried, using a running play, or passed into the end zone. Double the extra points for carrying/passing the ball into the end zone instead of kicking the ball over the end zone.

"Try" is not a cool word. "Go" is. Go for one. Go for two.

"Go for one" is a decision inscribed on the football scrolls. The scrolls found during some archeological dig in Alabama.

"After thou scoreth a touchdown, thou shalt kicketh for one extra point almost always unless thou art desperate and hath no choice but to goeth for two. Thou shalt not be different and try for two points regularly. If thou doth, people will thinketh thou art crazy."

Going for one is the decision that almost every coach makes. The decision that you have to make to be considered normal. It's the easy choice. The conventional choice. Passed down through the generations. A choice that is not understood or even agreed with, but a choice that is accepted for one reason — just because. Just because someone said so. Just because it's always been done that way. One of those decisions that is confused with being a rule.

"Class, welcome to Coaching 101. First, we have to learn some rules. After you score a touchdown, you kick for an extra point."

"Is that a rule? Do you have to always go for one extra point?"

"Well, ya, it's a rule... er, not a real rule... a coaching rule. You know what I mean!"

"So, can you go for two points?"

"Well technically, you can go for two. But that's only when you're desperate! For crying out loud, don't go for two any other time!"

"Coach, what's that banging noise?"

"That's me hammering it into your head."

Going for two is considered rogue. Counter-culture. Risk-taking. Going for two is the football version of high-stakes gambling. Even reckless. Why?

WIYF? (What If You Fail?)

The four words that put more fear into a person than any Goliath can. Life-altering words. Four words that keep you from moving, from growing, thinking, doing, from being. Four words that keep you out of the alley.

Going for two and failing brings out the critics.

"OOOOHHHH boy. That decision will haunt him!"

"It's too early in the game to go for two!!"

"OOOEEEE... that's going to cost them."

Criticism is dressed-up fear, delivered with one of the three S's — smile, scowl, or smugness. It's a type of elementary school public scolding. Finger-wagging, I-told-you-so. It's a marketing strategy for a club membership. An SSC membership. Scared Shitless Club.

"Twoferone deal today! Free membership to the Scared Shitless Club! Bring a friend! Bring several friends! You get a shiny new card! And, it's a LIFETIME membership! Join us. Be like us. All you got to do is two things. One, think the same as everyone else and two, criticize every person who tries something different and fails."

"Will there be free donuts and coffee?"

Extra point failure is not fatal. It's not an apocalyptic event — you simply don't get extra points. In fact, the word "failure" in relation to a missed extra point try is a misnomer. Six points were earned just a few seconds earlier. A touchdown is an accomplishment. Six points. A positive. A huge success. A missed extra point does not negate the earlier success. Missing the try for extra points is a small negative. Very small.

The decision to go for one or go for two has a paper-thin risk/reward gap. One risk is the consequence of earning zero points. The full range of the conversion reward is zero points to two points. In reality, not much of a gamble. The operative word is "reality." The game of football is not reality. Or, is it?

Football has a rigid culture of thinking. Strict traditional way of doing things. Plus tough talk. Real tough. Scary tough. Coaches use a special tough language. Smash-mouth. Blitz. Sack. And inspirational quotes.

Football coaches are born motivational speakers. Anything is possible. No limits. No fear. They can inspire the dead. The message is simple: Infinite potential. Everyone has limitless potential. The sport provides a stage to develop it, to show it, and to help others reach it.

One problem. The vast majority of football coaches are conformists. Extreme conformists. They fear doing anything that contradicts mainstream thinking. They fear making unconventional decisions. They fear having to explain outside-the-box strategies.

The evidence? The staggering volume of the automatic, copy-cat decisions: go for one instead of two; punt on fourth down instead of attempting a first down. All of these choices are paths of least resistance. The accepted path. Pleasant, familiar path. A bright, shiny path. Not some dark, scary alley.

The decision to go for one or to go for two will not affect world issues. The choice will not cure deadly diseases, feed the hungry, stop wars, or reverse a recession. The outcome of the decision will determine if the team that just scored the touchdown will earn a total of 6, 7, or 8 points. That's it. Failure to earn extra points will not bring on the four horsemen. The white rider will not warm-up if you go for two and blow it.

But there's a flip-side to the conversion dilemma. The extra point paradox. Going for two and succeeding earns you the "genius" label. Mensa club membership. Jarod — The Pretender. Moving a football three yards into an end zone gets your picture next to Einstein's. Theory of Relativity — Two Point Conversion. Same thing. And, you obviously have Novocain in your blood.

"He's going for two when he didn't have to! And he got it! Man, he's got balls!"
"No question, Billy Bob!! He has huge balls!"

To kick or not to kick. Genius or conformist.

Balls or no balls.

∞

"Coach, can we go for two? Remember what you said in your pre game speech?"
"Are you crazy?? WHAT WILL PEOPLE THINK!? No, we're kicking."
"But what about all that inspirational stuff? All that tough talk?"
"KICKER!! GET THE KICKER ON THE FIELD!"

In the football culture, there is no relationship between tough decisions and tough talk. Smash-mouth becomes softmouth. Run people over? Nah, kick the ball over their heads. Ta hell with smash-mouth.

"Coach, but it's fourth down and a nanometer." (The distance needed for a first down is the width of a credit card.)
"Can we go for it... just to show we have balls?"
"KICKER!"
"But coach... what about the smash-mouth speech? The part where we were going to cut through them like tanks?"
"JUST KICK IT OVER THEIR HEADS! DOGGONITTT!"

Blinking is silent. Blinking doesn't actually make a sound. No one can hear a blink. But blinking in the face of a Goliath-sized decision is powerful. A blink sends shock waves. It rips through the minds of those who believed the voice and in the mind of the voice itself. It breaks hearts. It hardens hearts. And, it cuts through souls. Blinking is soul-wrecking.

Blinking earns you an SSC membership card. The card that gets you a lot of company. No loneliness. Company with a lot in common. Drudgery. Boredom. Dread. Blinking conditions the mind to accept conventional thinking. Keeps you walking in the same direction in the crowded mainstream.

Blinking is the conformity-builder that smashes innovation. Dream-killer. It's a safe Pavlovian response that promotes more of the same. Blinking keeps everyone on the accepted path. The safe zone. The comfort zone. If you blink enough times, you lose yourself.

We don't enter this world as blinkers. We become blinkers. Who we are, who we become, depends on the number of times we blink.

∞

The distance needed to earn extra points is three yards. The ball is positioned only three yards from the opponents' goal line. Not three-hundred yards. Three yards. Nine feet. One-hundred-eight inches. Roughly the length of one-and-one-half football players. A person could stumble that far. Any ugly tossed ball could reach the end zone at that distance. Overhand. Sidearm. Shotput style. The ball has to travel only three yards.

An American football field has two metal poles, at the back border of the end zone, that form a U-shape. These are the "uprights." Not uptights. Uprights. The uprights form a designated space for the ball to pass through when kicked. The end zone is 10 yards long. On offense, the guy who holds the ball for the kicker lines up 7 yards behind the original placement of the ball, 3 yards from the goal line. The ball needs to travel a total of 20 yards, through the uprights, to earn one point.

The other team, the defense, lines up 11 nasty people who rush at the kicker trying to "block the kick." Minus the kicker and the holder, nine guys are left to block the 11 nasty defenders. If the kick is blocked, the defense is allowed to pick it up and run toward the other end zone. They'll get two points if they cross the far goal line.

If the offense decides not to kick, it can earn two points by calling a running or a pass play and traveling the three yards into the end zone. The same rule applies as with a "blocked kick." If the defense intercepts the pass or picks up a fumble, the defense can earn two points if they run the football 97 yards the other way.

Legally, the "try" is a chance for both teams to score extra points. An unavoidable risk inherent to any extra-point play. You can't escape the risk of the other team scoring even if you take the easy road — one-point try. The rule-makers made the conversion compulsory. If they didn't make the extra point play mandatory, coaches would probably not even bother trying to earn even one extra point. That would be the safest thing to do. Not even try. Eliminate all possible risk. But, the football legislators mandated trying. You have to at least try. Even if you just choose the safe path.

∞

A long time ago, someone said that kicking a football over the players' heads is safer than running through players or passing the ball over them. That person is unknown. Anonymous. But, he must have had a powerful voice. If you say something long and loud enough, people will believe it.

Kicking became the overwhelming consensus decision for the extra point. The same kind of kicking used in the anti-football sport: soccer. What should have long ago been the ultimate Culture Shock became the accepted, safe "go for one" decision.

"Kicking? Isn't that what them soccer players do?"
"Soccer will never catch on over here. Too much kicking."

The gentle path. One point. Kick the ball gently over everybody's head. Just like soccer.

"What? You're missing football practice for soccer practice? Are you crazy?"

The two-point conversion was born in 1958 — to add drama. The drama of the decision to go for one or go for two. Except that almost no one complied. Going for one continued to be the almost automatic play after a touchdown.

"Touchdown... Wally the kicker is jogging onto the field."
"This game is brought to you by... "
"Quick. Get me a beer and some chips. They're kicking the extra point."
"Get it yourself, Harriet."

How automatic? 95% of trys are single-point kicks. Only 5% are two-point conversions. Two-point conversions are only half as successful as single-point kicks. 95% of single-point trys are successful compared to 42% of two-point conversions. Why? Probably because two-point conversions are not practiced nearly as much as one-point kicks. Most likely, 95% of extra-point practice is devoted to kicking. Sports multi-culturalism. Soccer practice during football practice. What you focus on grows.

"Wait a minute... Where's the kicker? Holy mackerel Barney... He's going for two!"

When it becomes apparent that the rare (5%) try is about to happen, TV experts/announcers can be heard shrieking this announcement all the way to the next county, as if the coach just made a life-or-death decision.

"Ohhhh, this is a big gamble, Barney. I don't agree with this decision. It's too early in the game. No one attempts this so early in the game. This could be a disaster."

…the obligatory caution that follows the shrieking.

Big gamble? What big gamble?

"Gee Wally... a new brain surgery procedure is being tried right now. FOR THE FIRST TIME!"

For something to be a "big" gamble, a "big" consequence has to be a possibility. Death, for example. Earning six points instead of eight points does not qualify as a consequence. Doesn't even make the top 500 list of potential consequences. Extreme conformity skews logic. It causes the word "**genius**" to replace "**contrarian**," "**maverick**," "**balls**." The decision to "**go for two**" instead of one will not get you a climate-change Nobel prize.

How did this happen? How did perceptions get so out of whack? Many coaches have never had a real-life job. Many never leave the friendly confines of a football field or the artificial, insular world of academics. This internment shrinks one's worldview and expands pretentiousness. Tunnel vision. A narrow lens to view life through.

If you've never had to make a life-altering decision, then going for two instead of one can seem epic. You need a real-life job with real-life problems, as a point-of-reference, to position the "extra-point" decision where it belongs.

What causes conformity?

According to scientific research, the cause is human nature. A strong tendency to blindly follow — it exists in the majority of humans. The 66% conformity rule taught us that two-thirds of people conform to the thoughts and conduct of others even if they don't agree with the minority. Two-thirds will blindly follow others even if it means sacking personal beliefs.

A shocking example of this is Milgram's shock experiment. Otherwise normal people kept administering what they believed to be real electric shock to innocent patients despite witnessing obvious pain and suffering. In other words, even though they could see, with their own eyes, the agony that they were inflicting, they not only kept it up, they increased the voltage. Why? Simply because some guy said it was alright — the pain wasn't that bad — just keep turning up the knob. 66% kept jacking up the voltage even though they witnessed the subject's pain increasing exponentially.

Zimbardo's jail experiment simulated a prison. A mock jail with fake prison guards. The wanna-be jail guards were given some weapons and told to create a power-based environment. Jail guards were to have all the power. Inmates none. The experiment went so far out of control, it had to be stopped. Cut short before halftime.

The Asch Line experiment was tamer but no less profound. A group of people were shown different length lines on a chart and asked to identify the longest line. The entire group was composed of actors, except one person — the person being tested. The actors were told to lie. Over two-thirds of the test people followed along with the lie even though they could see with their own eyes that the line identified was not the longest.

Blind faith. Plus a dark side. Fear of being different. Fear of separating from the pack. Being right. Misery loves company.

The actual percentage of conformists is likely higher than 66. It's more like the drunk driver standard (over 80) or body temperature (98.6). Regardless, most football coaches think alike. Kick for one point after a touchdown. Punt on fourth down anywhere near midfield even if only 2 millimeters is needed for a first down. Kick a field goal on fourth down and inches in the opponents' area instead of going for it.

Eventually, you begin to believe that these decisions really are etched on tablets brought down by Moses. Or, written in the football gospels in some coaching bible.

∞

Someone designed the Hubble spacecraft that is flying around in the outer reaches of the universe — where the human mind can't comprehend. Someone designed the camera that they put on the Hubble spaceship. The camera routinely sends crystal-clear pictures back to Earth. Pictures from ectogizillion miles away. Hubble hasn't smashed into anything. The camera hasn't run out of film. What's so hard about moving a football three yards?

"Let's watch that touchdown again! Look at how that guy ran the ball past all those defenders!"
"And don't forget Ralph, they scored a two-point conversion right after!"
"THAT'S WHY THE COACH IS A GENIUS!"

Three yards. Nine feet. Nine giant steps. The length of Goliath lying on his back.

The only problem with three yards is the clutter of players. Twenty two players crowded into an area 53.3 yards wide by 13 yards long — from the line of scrimmage to the back of the end zone. Crowds sometimes get unruly. Eleven Davids running at eleven Goliaths, bumping into each other may cause chaos and confusion. But, it's still just three yards.

Use faster slingshots. Faster stones.

When you're down by two points with 4 zeros on the clock, the decision to go for two is a no-brainer. No genius title given for this decision.

"They're down by two, Barney. Last play of the game…"
"He'd better go for two or we'll have to call the authorities!"

When the decision is not a no-brainer, and it's not the last play of the game, coaches dust off the "two-point conversion chart."

A chart that no human can memorize. A chart that makes absolutely no sense.

"C'mon. Wally, where's the chart?"
"Here it is, coach!"
"Let's see… If you're down by one, go for two. Down by two, go for one. Down by three, go for one. Down by four, go for two. Up by…"
"TWEEEET… Delay of game… 10 YARDS… David!"
"Dagnabbit Wally!… Who made this chart???"

The chart has some mind-numbing formulas but what it doesn't include, can't possibly include, is the actual important stuff. Such as:

1. How much time is left.
2. The distinct possibility that the score may change many more times, thereby negating the formula that prompted the earlier decision.
3. All the unforeseen disasters that can dramatically alter a football game.

The chart is not contextual.

Regardless, no chart needed on this last play. No formula. No la top. Last play. Down by two. Go for two. The only question was "what call" to make — pass or run. And, which play specifically. A pressure-packed decision. Clock ticking. Miracle at stake.

But that decision was a no-brainer also.

Just remember the "lessons-learned" research that your life taught you. Remember what got you here. Think of the obvious. Common sense.

In this case, the answer was obvious. Pass. Spread offense style. No-huddle. Warp-speed. Spread out as many receivers as possible. Receivers sprinting all over the place. During the past quarter-century, this strategy worked just fine. Extremely well, in fact. It averaged 36 points per game at three different levels of competition. That's a lot of points at any level of football. Part of that success has been attributed by our decision to "**go for two**" 100% of the time and passing "**over 80**" percent of the time. Pass a lot and go for two every time. Two unconventional strategies. This meant that we invested over 80% of our reps practicing passing and going for two. Familiarity breeds success. The greatest emotion known to mankind is fear. The greatest fear is of the unknown. Over 80% of reps, passing, eliminates the unknown.

So far, this had been a typical game for the X-Men but an extremely unconventional one in the eyes of others. Four touchdowns scored and four two-point conversion attempts. Going for two 100% of the time is not heard of. Nobody goes for two that often. Not in one game. Not in one season. Going for two after each touchdown doesn't cause simple head scratching. It drops jaws. And causes… yelling.

"DOESN'T HE HAVE A KICKER?! "
"THIS AIN'T NATURAL!"

On this day, we made three out of four two-point trys. 75% success rate. Far above the average. Our score: 24+6=30. If we had gone for one and successfully kicked on each conversion attempt, we would have scored only 28 points — we would have not been in a position to tie the game. There would be no last play drama. In fact, there would be no last play at all. The rules stipulate that the extra-point play is unnecessary after time runs out if the play will not affect the final outcome of the game. 100% of 4 single-point kicks is not as good as 75% of 4 two-point trys.

24+6=30 Instead of 24+4 =28. It pays to "go for two."

"Pssst. Barney. Get this. Crazy Canadians. They don't kick."
"What? They don't kick? Why not? Don't they have kickers in Canada?"
"Dunno. Gotta find out though."
"Never heard of such a thing."

One play left. Down by two. Exactly what pass play to call to get the ball to travel 3 yards to get into the end zone. The Vatican was waiting. Forty seconds to make the right decision.

∞

Quick Gun Bravo 5, Mike 4, Delta 3… Bravo Charlie 8, 7.

In football, like in real-life, some calls are obvious. Unchallenging. Not mentally stimulating. No-brainer calls are just that. No need for the brain to do any real work. Second nature. Just make the call and move on. No pretense. No self-doubt. No self-importance. No grandstanding. No drama. Just make the call and move on.

What do we do well?

Pass.

What do we practice the most?

Pass.

What are we horrible at?

Running.

What passing strategy is best?

The same concept that we use over and over. Spread out the receivers.

Why? Not because we are geniuses. But because we've practiced it and did it repeatedly. Not because of magic or osmosis. Not by unexplained forces of nature. Because of reps. Over and over again. Repetitions.

Find something you believe in. Teach it. Learn it. Keep doing it. Fall down. Get up. Get knocked down. Get up again. There is no 10 count. No mandatory "3 knockdowns and you're out" rule. Eventually, you get good at it. So good that your knockdowns stop. If you practice long and hard enough, you cause the knockdowns.

What you focus on grows.

What you focus on a lot becomes monstrous.

∞

Quick Gun Bravo 5, Mike 4, Delta 3… Bravo Charlie 8, 7.

According to conventional wisdom, running plays are vital for football success.

"The next rule of Football 101 is you have to run the ball to win. You have to call a lot of running plays to be successful. Write that down. Hey… you in the corner! Are you getting this?"

Myths are like monsters. The more you talk about them, the bigger they get. A good running play gains an average of 4 yards. At that rate, it would take forever to score a touchdown. Passing gains substantially more yards, resulting in more points in less time. And no-huddle passing can tire out any Goliath. Any size. Any place.

That's why there was no actual "which play" decision to make for the last play. Send out all 5 eligible receivers to catch a pass. That leaves five blockers to protect the quarterback. 5+5+1=11. Unconventional. No one in the backfield except the quarterback. Risky. The quarterback is alone. It's called an empty backfield. It means minimal protection for the quarterback. Only five guys protecting the quarterback. Normally, it's six or seven.

The "spread" offense is like bad deodorant — less protection. But more choices. Less blockers but more guys running around trying to catch a pass from the quarterback. Give all 5 receivers individual paths to run. Make sure they don't run into each other. Have them equally spaced. Tell them to run as fast as they can. Tell the 5 blockers to protect the quarterback. Protect him like he's family. Fight to make sure he keeps standing. Do whatever it takes to make sure the quarterback does not get knocked down.

If everything works out, the quarterback throws the ball and a receiver catches it. In the end zone. Two points.

∞

Quick Gun Bravo 5, Mike 4, Delta 3... Bravo Charlie 8, 7.

A sentence in football language. The first part represents the formation — 5 receivers. Empty backfield. The second part is the frontside of the pass play. The primary side. The place where the quarterback looks first. The quarterback finishes the play by calling the backside — the rest of the play. The call takes one second to decide and about 3 seconds to yell to the quarterback. Only a fraction of the 40-second clock is used up. No time for Goliath to catch his breath. No recovery time. No rest between sets.

The 3 seconds could actually be eliminated because the quarterback has been instructed to call this same play over and over again.

"Listen... There's no sense in practicing hundreds of two-point pass plays. We use three. All three work but stick to one. Five receivers... Bravo Charlie eight seven. Because it works."

This "**spread**" offense was extremely unconventional until a few years ago. Too risky. A marked departure from the sacred football scrolls. Now it's a growing rage. One guy said it worked. Then another. Like a "**spread shock**" experiment. Monkey-see, monkey-do.

Quick Gun Bravo 5, Mike 4, Delta 3... Bravo Charlie 8, 7.

Great call. Awesome call. Yell it and watch it. Then move on.

Problem? There were some pesky distractions. The scoreboard for one.

∞

There are a number of reasons why a scoreboard can cause a problem. Cloud judgment. First, you might not be used to seeing a scoreboard during a game. Coaching football in Canada for over 30 seasons conditions you to not seeing a scoreboard. In Canada, you're lucky if you can find a decent football field. If you do find a level plot of grass to play on, there's usually no scoreboard — no time clock, no score, nothing.

The Canadian football scoreboard in an amateur game consists of a coach yelling to a referee:

"HOW MUCH TIME LEFT?"

A referee then stares at his wristwatch for a few seconds and yells back:

"FIVE MINUTES!"

What a coincidence. A neatly rounded-off number. This type of answer often causes an argument between the coach and referee to erupt.

"How can it be exactly five minutes!?"
"Watch your mouth coach or it'll cost you 15 yards!"
"Ya?"
"Ya!"
"Oh, ya?"

And so on... A time clock is essential for conflict management.

Figuring out the score during a Canadian football game is a test of short-term memory. It's not unusual to hear players and coaches calculating scores on the sidelines during the fourth quarter instead of thinking of more important things — like their assignments.

"It's 24-21, right?"

"No, I think, it's 25-20... Didn't they miss the extra point after their first touchdown?"

Finally someone yells:

"HEY, REF! WHAT'S THE SCORE?"

One of the officials eventually removes a crumpled piece of paper from his pocket and reads the score, much like the town crier in ancient Rome.

Can you imagine a hockey rink in Canada without a scoreboard? No, that would never happen. The culture wouldn't allow it. No scoreboard in a Canadian hockey rink would cause Culture Shock. Impeachment. Civil unrest.

And there was the temptation to take a picture of the scoreboard on the Crackberry. To help process the information and also to have a nice picture to hang up in the office. Plus you need proof. Miracles need evidence. 38-36 is so foreign, so completely unexpected, the brain will not process it immediately.

Research shows that the human mind needs to process 40 bits of information per second to understand what is being observed. The upper capacity for humans is processing 126 bits per second.

Depending on the mathematical perspective, it shouldn't be hard to understand a football scoreboard. But in extraordinary circumstances such as this, a processing delay is forgivable. Miracles disrupt thinking.

Reaching for a Crackberry during anything related to football (game, practice, film review) is a cry for help. Holding it borders on committing a federal offence. Using it — Culture Shock. And, it would be uncool. So, no picture.

The place you're standing is the second distraction. Especially when you're in their house, not yours. The United States of America is the home of football. Canadians are visitors, not occupants. Neighbours. Visitors don't feel at home. Nervous laughter. Backslapping.

"Use your manners, ya hear?"
"Yes ma'am."

"And follow their rules. It's their house."
"Yes ma'am."
"And eat whatever's offered to you. Even if you don't like it."
"Yes ma'am."
Neighbours control behaviour.
"You did what? What will the neighbours think?"
"Sorry, sir."
"Did you say hello to the neighbours?"
"Yes sir."
"Damn neighbours. They bought a new car!"
"Pardon sir?"
"Watch what you say to the neighbours, Biff. Watch what you say. I don't trust 'em."
"Yes sir."

If the place isn't home, there may be the tendency to become someone you're not. Out of character. Change your personality. Temporarily. Struggle to impress. Laugh when others laugh. Do things you don't believe in. Because you're in a strange place. A stranger in a strange place = strange behaviour.

These distractions were forgivable. The score shouldn't have been that close. It should have shown a gap — a gap just like in football culture. The football cultural gap. On the surface, it's real, but it's hard to explain why. Canadians are more familiar with American culture than their own.

In southern Ontario, we live and practice only a few miles from the border. We get Buffalo and Detroit TV stations. We watch CNN more than the CBC. We know that 270 is the magic number for the electoral college. We know more about Republicans and Democrats than we know about Conservatives, Liberals, and the NDP. We know that Arnold was the governor of California but we have no idea who the premier of Alberta is. We know who the vice-president of the United States is but we're not sure if we have a "vice-Prime Minister."

Football is part of the American culture, not the Canadian culture — not financially, physically, emotionally, or intellectually. That's why 38-36 didn't make sense to the brain. The gap was too narrow. Outside the comfort zone of the past four weeks — big gaps. The expectation of referees saying the neighbourly:

"We'll keep the clock moving for you, coach."

… referring to the great football contradiction. The "sportsmanlike versus insult" paradox. When the halftime score is out of control, referees intentionally shorten the game, by ignoring clock stoppage rules, in an effort to prevent an obscene final score. Less time in the second half, less humiliation for the losers.

"Thank you, Mr. Referee. Very neighbourly."

Translation…

Referee: *"Man, you Canadians suck. You gotta learn to play OUR game. We'll get you outta here quick. Back on the bus ASAP."*

Canadian coach: *"You pompous ass."*

38-36 also impedes the ability to make a call within the time allotted by the rules. Football is a time-restricted game. A game of clocks. A ticking madness — preventing the dreaded procrastination. No procrastination allowed in football. There's a game clock and there's a 40-second clock. The game clock keeps track of the time left in the game. 15 minutes, 4 quarters, 60 total minutes per game. A complicated set of rules determine when the game clock stops, when it starts, and when it keeps ticking.

Working the game clock is a big deal. Coaches call it "**Clock Management**." When you're getting clobbered, Clock Management is simple — keep the clock ticking and get the hell out of there fast. If possible, rig the clock during halftime to speed it up.

The 40-second clock is a phenomenal idea. It sets a limit on decision-making. Forty seconds to make a call between plays. That's it. As soon as one play ends, a clock automatically starts counting down giving the offense only 40 seconds to get the next play going. Forty seconds to make a decision and move on. If you go past that time, the referee throws a yellow rag to the ground and penalizes you for "delay of game." No screwing around. No meetings. No agenda. No oily coffee and week-old donuts that were scraped off the floor last night.

No sub-committees. No bullshit. The referee blows the whistle and spots the ball. Puts it down. Like laying down the gauntlet. Like saying, "Now what are you going to do?" Forty seconds to get teenaged boys to line up properly, to think, and to do something productive. Parents understand this challenge. Unforgiving, but it works. Good for the football legislators.

31

Penalty flags should be a federal law in every workplace. Meetings would require a guy in a striped-shirt attending every gathering. As soon as someone breaks out the powerpoint, a yellow flag would be tossed to the ground.

"TWEEEET... Delay of meeting, Management. Attempted murder by powerpoint."
"Hey, come on ref. Are you crazy?? Everyone uses powerpoint!"
"TWEEEET... Meeting misconduct. Yer outta here!"

Pretentiousness? Yellow flag.

"As director of directing..."
"...15 yards... Unnecessary pretense!"

Whining about how overwhelmed you are? Yellow flag.

"Man I'm SWAMPED!"
"...15 yards... Unnecessary whining!"

What about big decisions? The really important kind.

"The Slippery Spoon for the office Christmas party?"
"Wait a minute... How are we going to exchange gifts? Secret Santa?"

There is no exception to the 40-second clock for Culture Shock. No time for therapy. No time to hire consultants.

"Hey, ref. I have a note from my doctor. It says I have Culture Shock. Do I get more time?"
"No, coach. 40 seconds."
"I'll go to the Labour Board."
"40 seconds."
"Union grievance?"
"You're down to 30, coach."

No-brainer calls really don't need more time. Trust your gut. Your instinct. Intuition is powerful. It's built over time. Built by experience. It won't let you down — if you listen.

The right call would take 3 seconds to communicate to the quarterback. Three seconds to yell one sentence from the sideline to the field. One pass play. And then move on.

The game would be tied. Overtime.

But, a new voice tackled intuition and slammed it to the ground.

Late hit. Unnecessary roughness!

An unfamiliar voice. Caused by Culture Shock.

III
All Things Must Pass

"The greatest enemy will hide in the last place you would ever look."
- **Jake Green (in the movie "Revolver")**

Everything in football is big. XL, XXL, XXXL. Including the size of a coaching staff.

"My coaching staff is bigger than yours."
"Oh ya?
"Ya."

The notion of a one-man coaching staff in football is absurd. The first reason is the volume of teaching needed. No sport has the diversity of positions and skills. The second reason is appearance.

One, coach? What will the neighbours think?

Only one coach sounds crazy. According to conventional wisdom, it is. Except in the Niagara X-Men world. For years, it wasn't crazy. Worked fine. Got the intended results. A one-man staff has a number of advantages. No workplace stress, drama, gossip. No workplace jealousy. Not unless you want talk to yourself, fight with yourself, or stress yourself out.

"Did you hear what that sonofabitch did now?"
"How did he get that job? I guess it's not what you know..."
"Pretentious ass. I can't work with him."
"Incompetent bastard!"

There are more advantages. No torturous, mind-numbing meetings. Unless you want to commit powerpoint suicide.

"Ok. Now I'm going to show myself slide #80 with the neat sound-effects I added..."

No workplace mediators.

"Hello, Human Resources? I have a problem with myself."

35

No pretending to be interested in disingenuous conversations with plastic managers.

"I was a football star until I developed a confucktion..."

Plus, you can't get fired.

"I'm firing myself because of irreconcilable philosophical differences. However, I want to thank myself for the opportunity I gave myself to work with myself..."

Conflict management is easy with a one-man coaching staff.

"Doggonit, that pass play won't work! Call a running play!"
"You're stupid!"
"No, you're stupid!"

A one-man staff is healthy. Never mattered what anyone thought about it — in Canada. All of a sudden, now it mattered. Cross-border coachig staff-size envy. Looking across the field and losing count while trying to come up with the exact number of coaches on the opposing sideline.

One... two... three...

"Coach, Biff's tired. Want me to go in?"
"Whadayamean he's tired? Yes, go in."

One... two... three...

"You've got 12 men on the field, coach... this isn't Canada... hehehe!!! Just giving you a break so you don't get a penalty."
"Biff, GET OFF THE FIELD!"

Four... five.

"Is that a trainer or a coach?"

Pow! Culture Shock.

It's time to change. Time to get a large coaching staff. Just like them. Time to use a new leadership approach. A kinder, gentler style. Be invitational. Soften up and use the collaborative approach. Get the players involved in the decision for the final two-point play. Hopefully it will encourage some of the older players to join the one-man staff next season because they will like me better. Get players' opinions now,

4TH & HELL SEASON 1

right now, just seconds before the most important call of the decade. A call that could shock two separate cultures. A call that could seal the deal with the Vatican.

"Hey guys, what play should we call?"

∞

Humans are born to grow. We are supposed to grow — smarter, stronger. We're supposed to change. But, we can't change simply for the sake of changing. Change has to happen only when there is a need to change. Only when what was working is no longer working. Only when instability has developed. When change is necessary to do something different to re-establish stability.

Twenty-first century language has some strange buzz words — invitational, collaborative, change agent. The common sense that was taught by parents to children has suddenly become the topic of graduate degree programs, power-point presentations, and workplace socio-babble. We are bombarded with information. Words, images, events. Internet, e-mail, IPOD, cell phone. The RAM fills up every hour, every day. What happens when the RAM is full? An explosion? A meltdown? A lack of judgment?

Judgment is a fragile complexity. It's the great dichotomy. It can be a strength or a weakness. It can be a proponent or an opponent. Reality is the key. Actual reality counts though, not our perceived reality. The problem is that we usually let our perceived reality interfere with our judgment. That's why it affects what we do, what we become. The closer our perception of reality is to actual reality, the better our judgment. We have to recognize reality. But we create our judgment.

Judgment is tied to personality. Who we are determines what we decide; what we decide determines who we are. Experiences alone don't shape our personality. What matters is their effect. How we respond to what happens to us determines what changes we let in. We choose what experiences we let settle in our brain. We decide what experiences we let shape our minds — which ones we a low to influence us. We decide by what we focus on. We choose our personality. We decide our character. We can make our personality our ally or enemy.

∞

Coaching should come with a Surgeon General's warning:

"Coaching may be hazardous to your health. Mentally and physically. It may take years off your life."

Or,

"Coaching may cause premature aging, premature death."

Or simply,

"Coaching may kill you."

A normal coaching staff has 11 coaches — one head coach, three coordinators (offense, defense, special teams), and 7 position coaches (quarterbacks, running backs, wide receivers, offensive line, defensive line, linebackers, and special teams). Some staffs are larger, some are smaller.

But only one coach is extremely rare.

Why do we have only one coach? Three reasons — money, workload, time commitment.

First, most coaches won't work for free.

"How much are you offering?"
"Memories only. No money."
"Uh... ya. I'll get back to you."

Very few people work for free.

Secondly, most people do not have the stamina to teach unskilled players. Coaching is teaching — hardcore teaching. "**Position**" coaches are the backbone of a team. They teach skills. They teach the fundamentals — blocking, tackling, throwing.

But most coaches don't want to be a position coach. They want to be a "**coordinator**." The play-caller. They want to "**call plays**." They want to be a genius.

"Thanks for coming to this interview. How long have you coached?"
"Never. First time applying."
"Well, we need position coaches."
"Oh, no. I wanna be the Offensive Coordinator."

"Why?"
"So I can coach at a big university someday. I wanna call plays."

The desire to "**call plays**" is the reason why video games are so successful. Madden video games let everyone be a coordinator. Calling plays is much easier than teaching skills. It's more glamorous, sexier. Calling the right play fills a psychological void in some people's lives. It foolishly makes them believe they are smart, cool. This attention fulfills the approval-junkie need much better than the (lack of) attention from being a lowly position coach.

The title "**coordinator**" impresses wives, girlfriends, co-workers, guys in the bar, players. If you are a coordinator, you must be a genius. Otherwise, you wouldn't be a coordinator. The wannabe coordinators are guys who mistake video games for real football. Real football involves real humans. Every player is someone's son. They have to be developed physically, mentally, and emotionally. Play-calling has the lowest priority on the coaching job description.

Football has a caste system. The high-class recruit and the low-class recruit. Those who are elite, blue-chip, highly-sought after players and those who are not. Developing the football "low-class" player requires immeasurable strength. Patience to the core of one's soul. The type of teaching that sucks the life out of you. You have to go through both the good times and the bad during the player development process. Fairweather coaching is not coaching.

You can't love your players only when they do the right things, only when they score touchdowns. Only when they win. What matters is that a coach keeps on teaching, motivating, inspiring, and mentoring through the good times and, more importantly, the bad times.

"I won't be at practice tomorrow."
"Why not?"
"My mom said I have to go to my grandma's for supper."
"How old are you?"
"Nineteen."

The athletic developmental process is painful   for both the athlete and the coach. Pain management is the key. Tolerance. Developing a high threshold for pain is a necessity, not a luxury, when developing athletes. But the teaching/learning process is the most painful — the part the Surgeon General would want you to be aware of.

"I didn't hear a whistle! Why would you stop chasing the guy with the ball?? Would you do that in a game?"
"OHHH! So you want us to run until you blow the whistle!"

To avoid the pain of developing athletes, either find fully-developed football players or don't coach. Play golf, tennis, video games, fantasy football. But don't coach.

Play-calling doesn't matter if players can't block, tackle, throw, and catch. You can call any play ever designed but it won't work if your players have not mastered the basic fundamentals and skills. Conversely, when they do have the basics down pat, it doesn't matter what play a coordinator calls. It will likely work. Once players have mastered the fundamentals, get the hell out of the way and stop meddling.

Standing on the sidelines, during a game, watching unskilled players screw up can be a form of masochism, if you define yourself by the lack of skill of a teenager who is trying to make something out of his life. If you define yourself by the performance of teenage athletes, you will die a slow torturous death — physically, mentally, emotionally, spiritually. Conversely, if you don't define yourself that way, it's rewarding. Watching kids who couldn't find their way to the practice field, walk into the alley and go face-to-face with Goliath, is extremely rewarding. Even if the pebbles miss. As long as they get in the alley and bring the slingshot, something good will come out of it. The key to coaching survival is how secure you are. Are you secure with who you are, or is your self-worth connected to how many touchdowns a 19-year-old kid scores?

"Touchdown! TOUCHDOWN!"

There is nothing sadder than watching grown men jumping up and down hysterically on the sidelines, fists pumping in the air, rolling on the ground weeping... all because a genetically-gifted 6' 2" 230 lb. sprinter ran faster than all the non-genetically-gifted "**low-class**" athletes. Living life vicariously through a "**high-class**" player is awful. What kind of emptiness causes this?

Player development is a slow process. Very slow at times. The skill development curve is not a steep incline with rapid, over-night success. It is almost a flat-line. A low incline. Sometimes, barely a rise. Development takes time. Many Gen X coaches want/expect immediate gratification. When that doesn't happen, dissatisfaction, darkness, and despair set in. Eventually, emptiness. The type that leads to a shattered personality. The kind that leads to the "**C**" words.

"Cowards! Chickenshits!"
"You mean that kid over there who can't even shave yet??"

And then there's the commitment issue. A football season is time consuming. It's a full-time job. The difference between coaching and many "real" jobs is that the three workplace 'L's — loafing, lethargy, and laziness — are not tolerated. There is no down time when you coach football. No time for gossip. No surfing the Internet at your desk. No playing with your Crackberry during practice. No text-messaging. No YouTube.

No workplace drama to replace actual hard work. You can't get away with being a salary-stealer, working at minimum capacity. Coaches have to actually work — every second of every practice, every game, every film study session, every weight room workout. In other words, the bad work habits developed in everyday workplaces aren't conducive with the demands of mentoring student-athletes in a violent sport.

There are coaches and there are recruiters. Recruiting the high-class, genetically-gifted, ready-made, skilled, fully-developed player will make any coach look good. Real good. Stronger, faster, smarter players will make any play-caller look like a genius. Recruiting is the path of least resistance. It's much more attractive than developing players.

The Niagara X-Men specialize in a different path — a culture of open-admission player development. Open-invitation and growth opportunities to all who apply; not just for the elite who have already met lofty standards. Open-admission coaching and teaching is demanding. At times, downright painful because growth opportunities are not created equal. What is challenging for one person can be boring to another, and tasks that are mundane to some can build dreadful anxiety in others.

Open-admission teaching is the hardest type of instruction because of the group size and the skill gap. Growth opportunities have to be proportionate. They have to match the skill level of each student-athlete. This can be done but conventional teaching strategies won't pass the grade. Expert hardcore mentoring is needed to meet diverse needs.

Many coaches get fed up in the middle of a game or a season.

"These guys can't play... They're stupid... They're weak... They're slow... Chicken-shits..."

Correct. That's why you have to teach, teach some more, motivate, inspire, teach even more, yell. Motivate the dead.

"They won't practice. They won't work out. They don't love the game."

Correct. Changing bad habits in young people takes strength. Don't complain about that which you tolerate. You get back what you expect. Changing a young person's bad habits is not simple. It requires a message. A strong message. A powerful message. And, staying on that message. The problem is broken focus. It's easy to get off message. To get off track. It's easy to let bad habits surface. Turn your head. Ignore. To not change what needs to be changed. It's very easy to rationalize what's wrong with a young athlete and what's wrong with a team wit out trying to change it.

Coaching sanity demands a clear perspective of what constitutes success. Defining real success is a must. Real coaching success is not exclusive to what's on the scoreboard. Success depends on whether or not your players became better humans while they were with you. Even if it's just a little better. Show them what to do and give them an opportunity. Create memories.

That's the key. Contribute to their overall self-improvement. That's the real legacy. Players remember how far you took them and how you got them there more than they remember game scores. The only thing that matters is how much positive impact you make on them, so they can go out into the real world and make an impact. Today, on the field, doesn't really matter.

Those are the reasons for one coach. It's that hard to find committed, qualified coaches who will work their asses off for an entire season, when the challenge is overwhelming, when winning is not expected, when you can't take your eyes off the road for one second. No time off. Not one minute away from the required work. And no pay.

The "one-coach" staff was never an issue. Until now.

What will the neighbours think?

∞

Football is not quantum physics. You don't need decision by committee. Analysis can cause paralysis. Logic and experience-based intuition are all that's needed.

But you have to be careful of the 66% conformity rule. At least two-thirds are approval junkies who dissolve in the mainstream versus 33% original thinkers who do not fear being different.

Conformity is a powerful influence.

"What play should we call?"
"388, coach. We haven't shown them the freeze option all day. They'll be surprised."

He was right. In fact, it would be a shock. We hadn't shown them that play because it was ancient. It was a 1980s play that had been our centerpiece when we feared passing the ball. The accepted thinking was that passing was high-risk.

The freeze option was great. In high school. We repped it out over and over and over. Every practice from 1985 to 1992. Did it work? Yes. Anything works if you rep it out. Anything works if you practice it repeatedly until it becomes second nature. Nothing works if you don't invest reps.

What you focus on grows. What you neglect dies.

But now, 388 was like that old school friend you'd lost track of. Fond memories. But like the VHS recorder, its time had passed.

FREEZE OPTION? ARE YOU CRAZY?

The intuition voice was working. It sent the right message to the brain. The volume was on full blast.

FREEZE OPTION? ARE YOU CRAZY?

Thank goodness for a smart intuition. And the power of the voice. Thank goodness it shouted to the brain exactly what to respond to the player who recommended "388."

A no-brainer response. A great response.

FREEZE OPTION? ARE YOU CRAZY?

Our intuition voice does not care about feelings. It's an ally — a tag team partner. The voice gives you a script to follow. A simple script. One that can be easily communicated. No mistakes. All you have to do is trust it and have the balls to say it.

FREEZE OPTION? ARE YOU CRAZY?

Honest, effective, accurate, and expected. No one would have been shocked or insulted. 388 was crazy. In fact it was stupid. Madness.

Honesty out — honesty in.

"All we expect is honesty here. Look. Read for yourselves. It says so right here on the first line of our Code of Conduct! There's nothing more important than honesty on this team!"

St. Paul warned us about the futility of the mind, how it will get in the way of figuring out what to do next.

The pre-Culture Shock response would have been simple, blunt, honest:

"NO! Absolutely not! NO FREEZE OPTION. ARE YOU CRAZY? WE HARDLY PRACTICED IT!"

But... pow! Culture Shock!

"Good call. Send it in."

∞

IV
Crossing the Threshold

"When you look into an abyss, the abyss also looks into you."
- Friedrich Nietzsche

"What's your citizenship?"

American border guards rarely smile.

"Canadian!"
"Where are you going today?"
"Buffalo State College."
"Purpose?"
"Football game. I'm the head coach of a team that's playing their junior varsity."
"Your team's from Canada?"
"Yes."
"And you're playing Buffalo State College?"
"Yes."
"You know who you're playing, right?"

If the **"honesty out — honesty in"** rule applied at the border, it would have been great to simply yell:

"DO YOU KNOW WHO THE FUCK THEY'RE PLAYING!?"

But fifteen years in policing teaches you that this type of outburst pisses people off easily. Absolutely nothing positive happens from impulsive profanity-laced challenges and name-calling.

"Yes, we know who they are."
"Where's the team?"
"They're coming on their own... behind us."
"Are you bringing anything into the United States?"
"No."

Actually buddy, one thing — hope. Just keep sitting there in that booth all day, pissed off at the world. We're gonna bring a bunch of Canadian kids here, with hope — to make history.

45

Border Guard 1
Coach 0

Trash-talking at the border is one-sided. That's the law.

The border was symbolic. It was a threshold of hope. We crossed it.

∞

The drive to Buffalo State College was only five minutes away from the border. That didn't leave much time to think. Except for one thing — pass. Pass a lot today. We can't play defense. We can't run the ball. But, we can pass at warp speed. A lightning-fast no-huddle. Let's make it into a fitness contest. Line up as fast as possible, run pass plays as deep as possible, and let's see who quits first. Sprint, no rest, do it again. No rest.

Extreme. Extremely fast, extremely unconventional, extremely hard work. First one to get tired loses.

That was our only hope. Pass as often as possible, to every area of the field, to every receiver on the field. Make their defense gasp for air and vomit if need be. No-huddle spread offense. Maximum ball distribution. Techno-football without the lights.

But passing ain't smash-mouth football! You gotta run the ball to win games!

More effects of the 66% conformity rule. Someone a long time ago decided:

1. Running the ball is the manly way to play football — the "smash-mouth" way. Low risk.
2. Passing is the finesse way — entertaining, and sells tickets, but doesn't win championships. High risk.

Say something loud enough and long enough, and people will believe it. Even if it doesn't reflect reality. The **"ground and pound"** rugby-look-a-like running plays, where hordes of players crowd into each other in a disjointed scrum, is actually the manifestation of fear — fear of passing the ball. Fear of what is not understood. Uncertainty makes anything appear to be a risk. The run-oriented "**smash-mouth**" offense style uses the cover of the macho-man mask to conceal the fear of risk-taking — passing.

Football coaches like to use war analogies to inspire the troops. They are renowned for their Patton-like positive "**can-do-anything-you-set-your-mind-to**" ideology. Except when it comes to passing. Letting the quarterback throw a football scares them. Passing frightens snarling "smash-mouth" grown men.

"Ok, today in Coaching 101, we're going to learn one of the many golden rules of football. There are three things that can happen when you pass, and two of them are bad. One, an incomplete pass, and two, an interception. All together now, say it with me: There... are... three..."

The prophets who preached this gospel probably believed there were three things that could happen when you cross a street and two of them are bad — getting run over or being too tired to reach the other side.

The football gospels are ancient. They concentrate on consequences and ignore positives. The bad overshadows the good. They need revision.

New Gospels. Such as:

A: There are five bad things that can happen when you run the ball:

1. No yards gained.
2. Loss of yards.
3. Fumble.
4. The ballcarrier could be avalanched under a mass of defenders and have to be scraped off the ground onto a stretcher.
5. The coach who keeps calling these plays when the other team is obviously stronger could suffer from high cortisol levels.

B: When real dedication to the weight room is not part of your culture, absolutely no running play will work — none.

C: There are three things that can happen when you pass with a warp-speed no-huddle, and all of them are good:

1. You weaken a stronger opponent mentally and physically. It's the best way to fatigue Goliath.

2. Explosive results are produced by catching deep passes.
3. Explosive results are produced by catching short passes and sprinting really fast after each catch for huge amounts of yards.

∞

Football is the greatest contradiction of all sports. It's a manly, tough-guy game but it includes plays that resemble two sports that don't appeal to the tough-guy football community — rugby and soccer — running and kicking plays.

Running plays in football are the postmodern version of rugby. Very entertaining — if you're a rugby fan. And effective — if you have the biggest, strongest, fastest athletes. Just find the fastest guy on the team and give him the ball. If your team has Goliath at running back and Goliath's relatives blocking for him, you can run any play you want. The only problem is getting him through a huge crowd of defenders who clog his running lane. A sea of bodies smashing into each other resulting in a pile of flesh. A mass of humanity trying to stop one guy running with the ball.

Oddly, rugby doesn't get very high television ratings in the USA. Not one of the top 4 professional sports. Yet we are inundated with the top 10 football hits every night, every week. Watch any sports show. "Top ten violent collisions." The modern-day version of lions and gladiators.

"Highlight of the night... Biff smashes a receiver going over the middle... OHHHHH MYYY!"

"Pepino's Collision of the Game, brought to you by Pepino's Collision. Wally crunches the quarterback and... OOOOOOHHH, that musta hurt. June from Cheektowaga wins a new paint job."

Rugby, in football, sells. Blood sells. What bleeds, leads.

Then there is the kicking hypocrisy. American sport talk show hosts laugh at World Cup soccer.

"Soccer's not a sport... all they do is kick!"

But, in football, it's perfectly fine for a kicker to race onto the field, on the last play of the game, and kick the ball over the heads of all the tough guys who have been smashing into each other for the past 59 minutes and 59 seconds. The ball gently sailing between the uprights.

Three points. Then the kicker goes hysterical. Hyperventilates. Jumps up and down, rolls on the ground, weeps uncontrollably.

The kicker — the guy in the spotless uniform. The football equivalent of Mr. Clean. The stadium loudspeakers should blare out the Mr. Clean jingle as the kicker takes the field.

Mr. Clean gets rid of dirt and grime and grease in just a minute.

Mr. Clean will clean your whole house and everything that's in it.

Mr. Clean… Mr. Clean… Mr. Clean.

And, the biggest, most ridiculous contradiction of all, and we hear it all the time — the "game-winning" field goal…

"And now, the Jiffy Hot Dog Player of the Day — the kicker. Here's the re-cap. With one second left, in a bloody game where players were carted off with broken bones, torn ligaments, concussions, and other traumas suffered physically and mentally, watch as the kicker bounces onto the field and kicks the ball over the heads of 21 players who had been violently smashing into each other for 59 minutes, TO WIN THE GAME! Let's look at that game highlight again."

"Wow, Barney, that ball had distance. What a pretty sight. The ball sailing over the heads of all those big tough football players. Kinda serene-like, don't you think?"

These same people who weep with joy when a kicker wins a game with a last minute field goal bash World Cup soccer. They conveniently forget that the kicker never actually participated or contributed in the substantive part of the game — the part that got the team to within 3 points of winning. Three points. Half a touchdown. There is no sport that has the equivalent of half-a-real-score — that's what a field goal is. Three points, half of 6. When the players on the field fail to get 6 points by scoring a touchdown, call on a guy, who never actually plays in the real part of the game, to kick the ball over everyone's head.

"FIELD GOAL TEAM! Where's the damn kicker? Hey you, kicker. Stop combing your hair and go win the game for us. And stop waving to your mother, willya?"

Imagine this absurdity in hockey. You can't score on the goalie, so, remove the goalie, stand at the blue line and throw the puck over everyone's head for one-half a goal. Or if you can't score with a hockey stick, pick up the puck with your hands and throw it in the net for half a goal.

"The Leafs start in their own end with 5 seconds to go on the clock. The score is tied. Wait a minute. The Leafs coach just called for the half-goal play."

The goalie comes out. Some guy, who can't skate, picks up the puck, throws it over all the bloodied, toothless players' heads and into the empty net. That half-point breaks the tie.

"LEAFS WIN! LEAFS WIN!"

Sounds absurd? It is. Just like kicking — in the smash-mouth, rough-and-tumble game of football.

Why didn't the border guard say:

"Do you know who their kicker is?"

Because that wouldn't be intimidating.

∞

Hey, USA border guard… Do you know who THEY are playing?

This is who the Americans were playing.

1986: Jeff Benoit. The best Canadian running back in the history of the Niagara Region, a southern-Ontario combined-municipality that borders western New York. Jeff was the tailback at Port Colborne High School, a small school competing against giant-sized monster competition. Goliaths.

Jeff was a scoring machine. Handoffs, pass receptions, kick returns — get the ball in his hands, he scored. Jeff built himself into an unstoppable force by lifting weights every day, every week, for four years during his high school career. He lived in the weight room. He translated strength training into a scholarship at an American university, a CFL career, and finally, a strength coaching career.

David can change into Goliath in the weight room.

In addition to being the best running back in the history of the region, Jeff was our kicker. An accomplished soccer player. It was acceptable to have our strongest, fastest guy kick the ball because at the very least, he was not a "Mr. Clean." His uniform got dirty. He lifted weights. He built muscles. He built himself into a natural Goliath. He paid the price.

Third quarter. 2:11 left on the clock. Fourth down and 2 on the opponent's 33-yard line. Score: Us 21 — Them 3. "**Them**" was a Goliath high school team who had never lost to Port Colborne High School — ever. "**Us**" was a small school team in a big-school league — at our request. We asked to play the strongest.

History was in the making. Decision time. Go for the first down or kick a field goal. Try to get two yards by letting an unstoppable force run through the opponent. Or, let that same unstoppable-force player kick the ball over everyone's head.

Make a statement by pounding the ball through the opponent:

There is nothing you can do to stop us.

Or make a different statement by kicking:

We'll take the safe, easy way out.

"Field goal!"

The field goal worked. A beautiful field goal. A stunning arch of the ball. It split the uprights right down the middle then traveled at least 20 more yards. Best field goal ever. Textbook field goal. All the players watched the ball sail over them. Then… pandemonium. Hysteria. Wild celebration.

There's a rule in the X-Men code of conduct: No celebrations — ever. Act like you've been there before and will be there again.

Not celebrating after scoring is intimidating to the opponent. Celebrations are not intimidating. They are undignified. Celebrations piss people off. Especially the other team. Celebrations infuriate and motivate the opposition. Not celebrating sends a message to the other team — scoring is expected.

Jeff had never violated this rule — ever. He had plenty of chances to violate it because he was a scoring machine. But no celebration — ever. He had a streak going. A no-celebration streak. After every one of the average 5 touchdowns per game that he scored, he casually handed the ball to the referee and jogged away.

51

Ho-hum. No big deal. Been there before, will be there again. Promise. Guaranteed.

That was his message. He stayed on message. Never got off track. The no-celebration streak had been alive for a long time. Since Jeff's first game as a rookie in 1985. All the way up to his third touchdown in this historic game in 1986. But then the streak broke. It died. It was assassinated.

The 33-yard field goal against a Goliath was the catalyst for change. A change agent. A paradigm shift. Jeff went hysterical. So did the rest of the team. Jumping, hugging, yelling. Emotional train wreck. It was a shock. The no-celebration streak was murdered by a kick.

We won. However, at the end of this momentous occasion, the mood turned somber. Breaking news:

"We just kicked for the last time. NO MORE KICKING. We go for it on every fourth down. Anywhere on the field. And we go for two every time. Why? Because we bust our asses in the weight room! We don't bust our asses to kick the ball over people's heads! We don't embarrass ourselves with wild celebrations over kicking! See you Monday."

One streak dies, another is born.

The new streak. The "**No-Kicking Streak**." Two decades long. Extreme unconventional decision-making. Urban legend. Twenty years of no punting, no field goals, no kicked point-after, and no deep kickoffs. Plus countless onside kickoffs.

"Are you the guy who doesn't kick?"

Unrivaled counter-culture decisions: *"Go for it."* Always.

∞

"Go for it" is a term that in conventional football language means *"take a huge risk and try to keep possession of the ball instead of voluntarily giving up possession of the ball to the other team."* Go for a first down. Go for two points. Go for the onside kick. In other words, go for whatever everyone else considers a huge risk.

Football is a game of possession. The ultimate goal is to score more points than the other team, but you need possession of the ball to do this. No possession means no scoring. A long time ago, it was decided that a football team is neatly divided into three units — offense, defense, special teams. The offense *"has possession"* and is supposed to score points. The defense is supposed to stop this from happening. And, special teams is the transition unit — a change-of-possession unit — where possession of the ball is transferred from one team to the other.

"Tell you what... We've tried 3 times to get a first down. No luck. So, we're giving the ball to you. You give it a try. See how you make out. But, we're not just handing the ball over. We're going to kick it to you so you have to catch it way over there, away from us."

Example. The punt team is a **"special team."** The punt team politely gives up possession of the ball to their opponent by punting the ball to them. Voluntarily. The same applies to the kickoff team — when the kick is long. Don't try to re-gain possession. Very conventional thinking.

"Hi, I'm from Italy. Big soccer fan. I came here to watch some American football but it sure looks like our soccer back home. Lotsa kicking."
"Hey, watch it buster. Soccer is not like our football — in any way at all!"

The offense tries to score. The defense tries to stop the offense from scoring. Special teams govern the transition of possession from offense to defense. It's like taking turns with your assets.

"I own that TV right now. However, I will give you possession of it — freely. You can have it to watch for a little while. But you have to give it back. Promise?"

A simple change in thinking changes the performance expectation.

Think of the offense, defense and special teams as all having the same performance goal, same job. Not different jobs. Exactly the same — it's called **"2-Ps: possession and points."** The defense's job is not to stop the offense. Its job is to score. Get possession of the ball and score. Intercept the ball, pick up a fumble, score. As a last resort, get possession by preventing the other team from getting a first down.

Same with special teams. Their first job is to score, not to facilitate a gentlemanly transition of ball possession.

"But that's not realistic!" You have to kick on fourth down. If you don't, you're reckless."

"We can't get the first down! No sense in even trying. Let's kick the ball to the other team. Give it away. We'll try later."

Unless "**later**" never arrives. Unless it's too late. Unless time runs out.

"Dagnabbitt! Shoulda gone for it. If I had to do it over again, I'd go for it for sure."

Punting on 4th down, instead of going for it, is a strategy. A strategy that emerges out of fear. Fear of failing to get the first down and being pinned in your own end. Fear of trying. Fear of being different. Fear of criticism… from very loud critics.

"I heard about you! You never kick!"

Again, strategy gets confused with rules. What is law and what is choice? What is free will and what is not?

The line that separates what you can do and what you must do gets blurred. Eventually, alternatives disappear. Strategies and rules become the same. Like punting on fourth down. It's done so often, people think it's a compulsory rule. Etched on a tablet. Written on a scroll. You go for it only in obviously desperate situations. And only once in a while. No, make that next to never.

You go for it only when it's absolutely necessary. Because WIYF?

What if you fail? Failure to get it, if you go for it, sets the stage for Armageddon.

The white rider warms up. He's at the post…

Going for it is perceived as the ultimate high-risk low-reward strategy known to football mankind. But it's not. It's just that the perception of risk versus reward gets scrambled so that the real reward is unrecognizable — only the risks are seen. Just like in real life. Objectivity is replaced by forced subjectivity. Eventually, we all try to do only one thing — avoid risks. Don't even try for a reward. Just avoid the risk. It gets to the point where we can't even make an intelligent risk-reward analysis because we are overwhelmed with fear. WIYF?

And it starts when we gain admission onto planet Earth. We are told what constitutes risk-reward. By others. It's passed down through generations.

"You want to be what? A coach? Get a real job, son. You got to support your family."

If football culture governed society, we would cross a street once a year. Maybe. If the coast was completely clear. Actually, we would probably never leave the house. Never get out of bed.

"He can't go for it all the time for cryin' out loud! That ain't real football!"

Going for it should be the norm. It should never be the core of a streak.

Going for it is a challenge but not a risk. Sports are supposed to challenge us. Inspire us. Athletics is supposed to be the place where dreams happen. Where dreams become reality. Where the impossible becomes possible and conventional fears are beaten down, not hammered in.

Going for it speaks to every athlete's spirit. The athlete's heart. The athlete's soul.

Going for it sends a message. We worked hard. We are going to try for a first down. Try to recover an onside kick. You will not stop us.

Going for it means staying on message: Don't give it up. Don't relinquish possession. Keep what you've earned.

It means changing your risk-reward perspective. Don't let others dictate what is high-risk and what is high-reward. There's a reward in going for it that has nothing to do with points on the board. It's learning to be different. Working hard and then trying. Just try.

∞

Always going for it causes Culture Shock. Extreme Culture Shock. Makes people say crazy things. A league official once threatened to outlaw "**The Streak**."

"They have to punt… He can't keep going for it all the time!"
"But Commissioner, the rules say they don't have to punt. It's their choice… Go for it or punt."

"Doesn't matter. No one goes for it all the time. Everyone punts. So should they."

A type of Culture Shock that creates a time warp. Makes grown adults go back in time, to their childhood when they did absurd things.

Sunday, 7:24 am… You have… one new voice mail from phone number 905-555-0001…

"Ya. I was at your game last night. You're ruining the game by not kicking. 66-51 is not football. You have to kick. Kicking is a beautiful thing."

The Streak caused a grown man to walk to a pay phone, deposit a quarter, and make an anonymous call to defend… kicking. The fact that we won 66-51 by not kicking bugged the man so much, he got up early on a Sunday morning to make a call from a phone booth so it was not traceable. Or was he an escapee? Maybe he was on unsupervised leave.

∞

The death of Jeff Benoit's No-celebration Streak caused more change. First the start of a new streak, then the team Code of Conduct was officially revised. The "**No**" list expanded from 9 items to 12.

No swearing.
No disrespect… to anyone.
No complaining… about anything.
No laziness.
No first name basis with coaches or front office people.
No talking to referees.
No drugs.
No steroids.
No alcohol.
NO PUNTING.
NO FIELD GOALS.
NO POINT-AFTER KICKS.

There is ZERO-TOLERANCE for any violations of any of the above.

The No-kicking Streak promoted another extreme. The onside kickoff. The short, 11-20 yard kickoff. The anti-kickoff. At the start of the game, during the game. Became a habit.

"We will onside kick every chance we get. Why? Four reasons. To show balls. It's a rush. It's different. It stresses out the opponent. Be original. Do not blend into the mainstream."

The rules say that the kickoff can be any distance, but it has to travel at least 10 yards before the kicking team can take possession by recovering it. Sure, they can grab it before 10 yards, but they have to give it to their opponent. The return team can take possession any time they like after the ball leaves the kicker's foot. Long kickoff, short or in between, it's the kicking team's choice. The rules say so. Do whatever you please.

"Take out your Coaching 101 textbook and follow along with me on page 2, the kickoff section. You must kick off long and deep. Now, I know it doesn't actually say that, but you'd be smart to forget about the part that says the kickoff only has to travel a short distance of 10 yards and just do the same thing as everybody else does. Kick off long and deep. Ok? There will be quiz right after the break. Hurry back."

All kickoffs are "**live**" meaning that when the ball is in the air, no one has possession of it. Therefore, a kickoff is open season. Either team can take possession of the ball. But, they have to fight for it. A short, onside kick is easier for the kicking team to recover. They only have to sprint a short distance to get the ball.

Long kickoffs? The returning team has the distinct advantage. No one on the kickoff team will outrun the ball to the kickoff return man. The ball always wins the race on long kickoffs. Generally, the only way for the kickoff team to recover a long kickoff is to hit the return man hard enough to cause a fumble and then recover the fumble. A long kickoff is the polite way of intentionally giving up possession of the ball.

"Look here. We just scored. It's only fair that we give the ball to you so you can have a turn at trying to score. But we won't just hand you the ball. We're going to kick it long and deep. As long as you hang onto it, it's yours. Deal?"

Sprint only 10 yards. Run into a bunch of people. Find the ball. Jump on the ball. Possession. Simple. Another chance to score. Recovering an onside kickoff is a big deal.

"But what if we don't recover the ball, coach?"
"Then the defense has to get the ball back and score. 2 P's... Remember?"

The fear of failure is overwhelming. Failure to get the ball on an onside kickoff is the worst nightmare.

What will the neighbours think?

"Now look how close the ball is to your end zone. You went for it and didn't get it!"

Suddenly the defense is forgotten about. If your defense is strong, it doesn't matter where they get the ball. If your defense is lousy, it doesn't matter where you get the ball. Either way, it doesn't matter, because a strong defense means you will get the ball back. And a weak defense means the other team will score regardless of where on the field they start from.

A strong defense is like a brick wall. A weak defense is a swinging door. Or no door at all.

∞

Conventional football wisdom teaches you to blink. It teaches you when to blink, how to blink. And to blink hard.

Group blinking. Lock-step blinkers.

Tough decision? Blink.

Tough situation? Blink.

"All together now... Ready, set, BLINK!"

A world of blinkers.

But always going for it makes adrenaline junkies. Addicts. A need to fight boredom. More excitement.

Never enough action. More need for a rush. It's never enough. "Enough" is taken out of your vocabulary.

No adrenaline rush? Now there's an apocalyptic event.

The white rider is at the post...

∞

People thought the No-kicking Streak was crazy. Except those that mattered — the team. The streak not only had a life of its own, it had its own DNA code. It became family.

Don't mess with family.

Watch what you say to players! Watch what you say. Not only do they buy-in to the unconventional, they expect it. Can't blink. Blinking is no longer an option. Can't back down or they think you're a blowhard like everyone else.

Who cares what the neighbours think! Who gives a shit!

Once a team has bought-in, it becomes a real team. No blinkers allowed. They believe you. They'll run through a wall. Any wall. As long as you don't blink. Do what they expect. When it's time to walk the talk, do not blink. Otherwise, they will believe you are a supreme bullshitter. Tough talk. No balls.

"Go for it. Right coach?"

A leading question that means:

"Don't blink. Don't take away the adrenaline rush. Don't back down. Don't worry. You taught us well. We believe we can do this. We have balls. We want to experience a rush, be different, and cause stress."

The NSSC. Not Scared Shitless Club. All players want a membership. To be part of something different. They want to experience the rush of doing something that no one else does.

But, non-members want to close down the club.

"Hell, if WE don't do it, no one should."

The non-members will try to pollute the members.

"You can't go on like this, fellas. He's leading you down the wrong path. Y'all gotta kick."

But a team's buy-in is powerful. It is contamination-resistant. A pollution flak jacket. Culture Shock immunity. All you have to do is one thing — don't blink. Don't back down. When a team accepts extreme unconventional thinking, extreme unconventional strategies, then no-brainers are created. Expectations are solidified — etched in stone. No more choices. You have to do what you said you would do.

Say what you mean, mean what you say.

Otherwise, you get classified as a bullshitter. Blinking makes you a bullshitter.

The Blinking Bullshitter… coming soon to a theater near you.

Twenty years is a long time for a streak. Joe Dimaggio's famous hitting streak lasted only 57 games. His streak ended because he struck out. Not his choice. He didn't blink. He didn't kill it. Our streak ended differently. Our streak died. It was killed. Homicide. Murder.

"Cause of Streak death?"
"Culture Shock."

In Buffalo, New York. While miracles were happening. David blinked not once. Not twice. Three times.

First blink: 4th down.

"PUNT!"

Second blink: Five kickoffs — everyone long. Long and deep. No onside kickoffs. Not one short, 10 yard, onside kickoff.

"Onside kick. Right, coach?"
"NO! KICK IT DEEP! As deep as possible."

Then. 388. A freeze option running play instead of a pass play.

Blink… Blink… Blink.

All things must pass. The No-kicking Streak passed away because we didn't pass. We had officially crossed the threshold — to the conformist, conventional world.

"Welcome to the SSC. The Scared Shitless Club. Here's your membership card. What will it be then? Day pass, month, year? Probably a lifetime? Right? What shall we put down as an expiry date?"

66% plus one.

∞

V
Sudden Death

*"All truth passes through three stages. First, it is ridiculed. Second,
it is violently opposed. Third, it is accepted as being self-evident."*
- **Arthur Schopenhauer**

"Laugh now, you asshole!"

Our team code of conduct specifically states, in bold print, "zero
tolerance" for disrespecting a referee. All communication with referees
is strictly prohibited — with two exceptions — team captains and the
head coach. That's it. No one else talks to, let alone curses at, a referee
regardless of how frustrating the situation. If communication with a referee
is necessary, the player must address the official as "Sir." Repeatedly. No
complaining to the ref, no whining, no wise-ass comments, nothing.
Ever! No exceptions.

Except this time.

It's easy to ignore a player yelling, *"Laugh now, you asshole!"* at
the referee the moment we scored to make the score 38-36. Pretend you're
busy. Look around like you're searching for something. Should have acted
disgusted. Should have admonished the impulsive disrespectful outburst.
But that would have been hypocritical. I caused it. Inadvertently. With
a pre-game speech. Players actually do listen carefully. And, they are
intensely loyal. Besides, the referee didn't hear it. Too much commotion
on the field.

The official wearing the white hat is the guy in charge of enforcing
the rules of a football game. He gets to throw a yellow flag to signify a
penalty. Football has a strange justice system. There is no due process.
No trial. Instant justice. The referee is police, prosecutor, judge and
jury. He makes the allegation and he convicts. No hearing. No defence
lawyer. Sentencing is measured by territory — in yards. Infractions
result in field position change. They move the ball five to fifteen yards,
depending on the severity of the penalty. Ejection from the game is the
football version of capital punishment.

Unlike real-world justice, football justice sometimes evokes heckling. In a real-life courtroom, heckling a judge gets you incarcerated for contempt of court. In football, you either get a warning, another penalty, or ejected.

∞

"You stunned ass!"

It's amazing what the conscience will do after you make a stupid decision. 388. Three simple digits. Three eighty-eight. First, the conscience stirs up nasty feelings inside your guts. Then, it tightens and ties up everything inside you. Makes a mess. Pressure. Tension. Anxiety. Every ailment known to mankind. The conscience leaves nothing to chance. Finally, it makes you talk to yourself. Out loud. Impolite self-dialogue. Nasty one-way conversation. A type of self-loathing.

The guy wearing the white hat was standing only a few yards from our sideline.

"Watch yourself, coach!"

It's not easy to convince a football referee that you're talking to yourself. It's not easy to admit to anyone that you are trash-talking yourself.

"I was talking to myself, sir."

Use some common-sense ref. You didn't do anything wrong. Why the hell would I call you a "stunned ass?"

We had just scored and were getting ready for a two-point conversion. Technically, we were happy. Miracle #2 had just happened. Why would anyone heckle a ref after a miracle? Referee-heckling occurs only when the ref pisses you off. The ref's warning was unnecessary. It should have been obvious that I was talking to myself.

No flag. He must have believed it. He turned to run (plod?) to spot the ball for the two-point conversion that would decide the game. But, there was that smug look — again. The same look all game long. The kind of look that gets locked into long-term memory. It started with the excruciating pre-game ritual — the "official introduction" with the officials. The first of several meetings with the refs.

The referee has a crew of officials. They wear black hats. About 15 minutes before the opening kickoff, they walk with the guy in the white hat, in a disjointed group toward the head coach of the opposing team — like a posse. The only things missing are the horses and tumbleweeds. It's a scene out of a bad western. The head referee thinks he's the sheriff. He usually has his hands on his hips. The other guys are the Barney Fyfes. You expect them either to draw their weapons or warn you to leave town before sundown.

Then it starts.

"They let you cross the border, eh? (Yuk, yuk.)"

The proverbial *"eh?"* That's original.

"Yes, sir. They let us cross. (Ha, ha.)"

Handshakes and guffaws all around. The only thing missing is a bartender and a rousing, *"This round's on me."*

"You're having a rough season, EH? (Chuckle, chuckle, yuk, yuk.)"

The second *"EH?"* is always louder than the first. The volume increases with each subsequent *"EH?"*

"Yes, sir, but we'll survive. (Ho, ho, ho.)"

Why do grown men have to use phony laughter to validate an introduction? Is insincerity mandatory when male people meet?

"I ref'd your game with St. John Fisher two weeks ago. You knew they were ranked in the top 10, right? (He, he, he)"

No, you idiot. We don't have telecommunication in Canada. Too far north. No Internet, no email. Cyberspace doesn't reach us. It can't cut through the snow.

"Yes, sir. They sure do have a great program."

Then, it develops into full force. The football comedy show! Starring: the obnoxious American referees wearing the unflattering tight striped clothes that make them look like constipated zebras.

"You know you can't play with 12 guys, EH? (YUK, YUK, ho, ho.)"

The whole crew has to laugh along with the head guy. Sad. Grown men attempting to shove their heads up the head guy's ass. At least there was enough room.

"Yes sir… 11 guys only… I'll try to keep that in mind."

Humility is allegedly a proactive strategy intended to prevent major conflict — externally and internally. Not with officials. Being humble doesn't help. Self-deprecation solves nothing. It only promotes rapid-fire sarcasm about the unexplained difference in football rules between Canada and the United States.

"What do you guys do with the 12th guy anyway? (He, he, he.)"
"Betcha you'd play better on ice!! (Ha, ha, ha.)"
"You guys have a single-point rule, don't you? How does that work? (He, he.)"

Now they're laughing so hard they're holding their bellies — to keep them in place. Kinda like Santa in pinstripes.

"You guys sure do have a BIG FIELD. What do y'all do with that extra space up there?"
"Y'all still line-up one yard off the ball, right? (Ha, ha, ha, ha,). Whose idea was that?"

Hey, asshole, don't forget the obligatory, *"How does all that motion work up there in the CFL?"*

"How does all that motion work up there in Canader anyways?"

Man. Imagine the Canadian outcry if Americans put 7 players on the ice at one time instead of six. We already scoff at the XXL-sized, wide-screen-like Olympic ice surface used in European hockey.

"Those Europe rinks are too big! Too much ice! Too much room to avoid stick swinging to the face and running players head-first into boards from behind!"

Yet, a citizen-led revolt would erupt if Americans bastardized the sanctity of our Canadian hockey.

We see it as cultural preservation. That's how Canadian football apologists rationalize changing the sacred rules of American football.

Three downs instead of four.

110 yards field length instead of 100.

A wider field — by 12 extra yards.

A longer end zone — twice the size.

Unlimited motion.

One-yard neutral zone.

Neighbours versus neighbors, fighting over size.

And, the worst change of all is the dreaded *"single point."* That's the one that puts the Americans over the edge. The single point is a reward for failure. Miss a field goal? We'll give you one of the possible three points, if you kick the ball out of the end zone instead of where the hell it is supposed to go — through the uprights. This madness is called a *"rouge."*

"Let me get this straight. If we have the ball on your 10-yard line and the game is tied with two seconds left in the game, all we have to do is punt the ball out of the end zone and we win?"
"Yes."
"The ball doesn't have to be place-kicked?"
"No."
"The ball doesn't have to go through the uprights?"
"Correct."
"We would get one point and we would win?"
"That's right. Punt the ball anywhere out of the end zone and we Canadians give you a single point."
"Hmmmm. And, if we try a field goal and miss, we still win?"
"Yup. If the field goal fails and the ball goes out of the end zone like it obviously will, you get one point for failing."
"Damn. That's some crazy-ass stuff. And you call it what??"
"A rouge."

A cultural metaphor.

Ah come on, so they missed the field goal, so what? Let's give em one point. They tried so hard. Their self-esteem might suffer.

A reward for failure in one country; no tolerance for failure in the other. Americans are right. It is absurd. And laughable. Same continent. Different rules. Senseless. On the other hand… It does fit the pattern. Miles-kilometers. Pounds-kilograms. Dollar-79 cents.

When the officials' obnoxiousness reaches the boiling point, it's time to pretend there is a crisis over where your team is warming up.

"Hey, you over there. You broke your route at 5 yards. You're supposed to break at 6!"

This pathetic strategy never works. The attempted diversion. Pretending. Yelling at a player for a fictitious wrongdoing in a desperate attempt to end the mind-numbing dialogue with the refs. The refs just get worse. Now the entire crew competes for the top comedian/social philosopher award.

"How come your taxes are so high? You don't even have a big defense budget."
"At least you have fully-paid medicare."
"Boy, your gas prices are a killer. My aunt's sister's son's next-door neighbor lives somewhere near Toronto. Pays double what we pay. How do y'all figure out what to pay? How big is a litre anyways? And, you have that different kind of money. Is it worth anything?"
"Well, y'all win at beer-making."

Consensus, heads nodding.

"Y'all make better beer than us. Did yous bring over any of that Labatt's?"

Finally, they close with nostalgia. Reminiscing about the good ol' days. Every ref has at least one fond memory of Canada as a recreational hangout.

"What's the name of that bar just outside of Fort Erie… used to go there all the time?"

How the hell should I know what bar you drank like a fish at!?

"That beach up there… Crystal beach… still open? Some hot women, boy, lemme tell ya."

ENOUGH!

"Look, I gotta get back to my team. Anything else?"

"You got any questions, coach, the side judge is Mike. He'll help you out with the rules."

Great. Just have him talk real slow so I can understand.

"Thanks, we'll be fine."

"Oh, and don't forget. If the score gets out of control, we'll move the clock along."

"That's kind of you, sir."

∞

You don't know the effects of what you say, when you're saying it. The **"Law of Unintended Consequences"** applies to everything. Including pre-game speeches.

"GET IN HERE!... LISTEN... LISTEN TO ME! I HAVE TO LISTEN TO THESE ASSHOLES LAUGH AT US BEFORE EVERY GAME! THEY THINK WE'RE PEACE-KEEPERS FROM SWITZERLAND! THEY THINK WE'RE SCANDANAVIANS WHO HAVE NO CLUE WHAT FOOTBALL IS. THEY BELIEVE WE'RE FROM FINLAND... NORWAY... SWEDEN! THEY THINK WE'RE A BUNCH OF SLAPDICK SNOWMEN! YOU HAVE NO CHOICE TODAY — NONE!! IT STOPS HERE. TODAY. YOU... ARE... NOT... SECOND... RATE... HUMANS!"

The **"us-against-the-world"** bit does not motivate or inspire. But, the **"second-rate-human"** thing does. You just can't break it out every game. Be careful of overuse. And, when you do bust out with it, you have to get red-faced. It has to be real. You have to mean it deep down. Real deep. As deep as you can go. There is no such thing as too deep. Authenticity is the key. When it's done right, players will go through a brick wall.

And, they'll never ask why. They won't need a ladder. They will stretch themselves far beyond what they ever thought they could. Unconditionally.

Why? It's the ultimate way to say to your players, **"I care. You're important."** It's a powerful way to lead, to motivate, to inspire. Telling someone that the goal is to become a **"first-rate human"** clarifies your role. It removes any guessing and all misinterpretation of who you are.

You can't impress young athletes with titles and knowledge. You can't simply tell them you're the leader. Players don't care about what you know or who you are until you show that you care about their journey. Until you prove you care about what matters to them. That's what separates leader from boss. Leader from manager. Leader from supervisor. It separates leader from cheerleader. It connects leader to coach.

Solve someone's biggest problem and you're a leader. Show them the way when they're looking for a way out of where they are. Real leadership is about bringing people out of their worst predicament. Whatever that may be.

Real leaders don't put up obstacles. They are not brick-layers — they don't build brick walls for people to crash into. They put up ladders for others. Ladders to climb — to their full potential. The real leader helps others perform at their best and doesn't worry about winning popularity contests. Leadership is not about feeding the approval-junkie addiction.

Leader and boss are not the same. There are only two real bosses: Bruce Springsteen and George Steinbrenner.

Leader and manager are not the same. Leaders bring people to the next level. Managers manage collective bargaining agreements and policies that keep people at the same level.

Leader and supervisor are not the same. Leaders thrive on the success of others. Supervisors dismiss success unless it's their own.

Leader and cheerleader are not the same. Leaders show others how to get rid of weakness by empowering them. Cheerleaders applaud weakness by enabling.

The best leaders are multi-taskers. They can kick your ass and make you feel important at the same time.

∞

Just minutes before kickoff, the guy in the white hat saunters past our bench with two guys in black hats. The smug look. Referee meeting #2. All their trash-talking before — they were just warming up. It was all above the belt. One more shot. The head ref couldn't resist. The low blow.

"Now, coach, do you need me to remind you not to kick on third down?"

Roaring laughter. White hat and his crew believed they had something on Seinfeld. They were ready to submit a sitcom pilot to the network executives. Maybe a Vegas act.

The "**three-down**" joke. Every ref has to slip in that one last cheap shot. Blind-sider. When no one's looking.

Have a good laugh, assholes… until you see the Streak.

The Streak shuts them up. It turns off the applause sign. Quiets the laughter. The Streak brings on silence. Never kicking is as far outside-the-box as you can go. There is no place farther. It is the outer reaches of outside-the-box. Even the starship Enterprise can't go beyond it. The smug look changes.

Bang — Culture Shock. Powerful enough to change smugness to silence.

The Streak evokes two types of commentaries.

"Gotta hand it to ya, coach. You guys have balls."

That's to your face. Behind your back it's different.

"Did you hear about the guy who doesn't kick? What's wrong with him? He must not know much about special teams."

Wrong. Just the opposite. After you've spent several years as a special teams coordinator, you become acutely aware that the punt team is the toughest part of football for both coaches and players. Why? The punt unit starts as an offensive team and converts in mid-play to a defensive team. Punt team players have to be both expert blockers and expert tacklers. The punt team needs 11 two-way players. An enormous amount of practice reps are needed to perfect the punt team.

We don't have that time in our reality. We're the St. Jude of football. Unheard of challenges. Limited practice time, limited number of coaches, limited everything. So, you make the best of the situation and you focus only on offense and defense. Not special teams.

"Let's see what he does on 4th down on his own 10-yard line. Let's see if he'll still go for it!"

We do. No choice. Expectation plus demand. Players expect it. They demand it.

You said it, let's do it.

There is no compromise with players. Their depth of buy-in and loyalty is limitless.

And, they handle Culture Shock better than coaches. Better than grown adults. Why? Because they believe you when you tell them that they can truly do anything they put their mind to. They will believe in the unbelievable. You can knock out the previously injected negativity that life has polluted their minds with by asking one simple question:

"Who did this to you?"

They put up their hand, just like in grade school. They answer the question. They tell you who contaminated them with negativity. They rat out their dream-killers. The hit-men who try to assassinate their dreams.

Deep down, players want to make a mark. Their personal mark. Their unique narrative to spread through the ages. They want their own "**you should've seen us**" stories. Something that separates them from the pack.

Players are starved for inspiration. They want to believe they are real warriors. They're simply waiting for someone to tell them they are. It starts with a bold statement. Bold statements are memorable. Especially when the listener has been waiting for someone to say something different.

"LISTEN TO ME CAREFULLY. THIS IS LIFE-ALTERING. THIS WILL DRAMATICALLY CHANGE YOUR LIVES."
"We never kick — ever. We don't practice a punt team, field goal team, or point-after team. We need a kicker for one reason — to kickoff. And, even then, he's not a kicker. He's a defender, a tackler. Not some spectator who kicks the ball then runs away."

People will ask you why we don't kick. Tell them:

1. It's a 20-year Streak. Hundreds of players have kept the Streak alive. You will not be the ones to break it.
2. We once successfully got a first down on 4th down and 15 from our 2-yard line. It's been done by your predecessors. It's worked. If past teams have done it, you can do it.

3. It's like jumping into the deep end with no life jacket. Swim or sink. NO CHOICE. NO OPTION. Not having a punt team makes you get stronger on both offense and defense.

4. Going for it on 4th down is not a life and death issue. Real-life will be harder than 4th down and 15 from your 10. Going for it now teaches you how to go for it on 4th down in real-life. How to deal with EXTREME ADVERSITY.

5. Going for it grows balls and it shows balls. Growing balls and showing balls intimidates the opponent.

6. It teaches you to be original. Don't blend into the mainstream.

7. It pumps adrenaline. Makes you feel alive.

8. If you can't get a first down, you have to get better.

9. If you don't get the first down, the defense will just have to get the ball back.

Our kicker will be busy enough without punting and field goals. Our goal is to kickoff at least five times per game. Achieving that goal shows we are meeting our 36 points-per-game average. And, we will onside kick at the beginning of the game; not just at the end. Our objective is the 2 P's — possession and points. That's why we onside kick over and over again in the first half. To build up the score so that we don't have to onside kick at the end of the game in desperation.

Exhibit A: 1994-1995. A new Canadian semi-pro team that went undefeated and averaged 48 points-per-game. Our kicker came to every practice. Had a canon leg. Amazing distance. Boomed every kick. He was signed by the Toronto Argonauts even though he never scored a point for us. Zero points. Not one. He kicked off eight times per game then ran downfield to tackle the return man after every kick.

That's how we do things.

Instant temporary buy-in is easy. Players immediately believe. They get pumped. But, buy-in longevity needs the next step — not blinking. Not blinking creates a legacy. It becomes legendary.

But so does blinking.

∞

Two blinks in 20 years threatened the Streak. "Blink cover-up" saved my ass. Salvaged the Streak. Two different quarterbacks committed Blinkgate. Covert operation. Preserved my "**authenticity**."

Both quarterbacks developed into amazing passers, but more importantly, they were real leaders. Balls of steel. Unselfish. Loyal. 100% committed to bringing their teammates to the next level. Unshakable.

First blink: 1995. On our 2-yard line. 4th and 12. In Canada. Timeout called.

"The Streak's over, Jay. We have to punt."

With who? We don't have a punter?

"Sorry, coach. No punting."

Jay ran back on the field, called a pass play, and got sacked in the end zone. Intentionally. He never got sacked. Our protection was better than the Secret Service. Smart man. He salvaged the Streak and our dignity. My credibility. And it only cost us 2 points. Getting sacked in the end zone is a defensive score. It gives the other team 2 points. More importantly, giving up the 2 points meant we had to kickoff — not punt. The Streak had been on life support and lived on even though I had my hand on the plug. But the message sent to the other side was clear:

"Holy cow! They're nuts!"

No one else had heard me blink or saw me blink. And, Jay has never told anyone to this day. Erased the tapes. Took the 5th.

Second blink: Two years later. 4th and 15 from our own 2-yard line. In Canada. Timeout. The "**rookie quarterback sensation**" ran to the sideline.

"The Streak's over, Tom. We have to punt."

With who? We don't have a punter?

"Sorry, coach. No punting. YOU TAUGHT US TO HAVE BALLS!"

Smash! That was a shot to the head.

Tom ran out to the field. Called his own pass play. Completion. 17 yards. First down. Crowd went nuts. Drove the rest of the field. Four minutes later — touchdown. No wild celebration. Streak saved. Streak suicide averted. Dignity intact. Bigger message sent. No one else had heard me blink. And, Tom has never told anyone to this day. Erased the tape. Took the 5th.

Two strikes. Two swings and two misses. Two swings at the Streak with a big bat that tried to bludgeon the Streak to death. But two misses.

"Another swing and a miss. 2-0 count. The windup, and here's the pitch..."

Strike three and you're out.

Blinked in the United States of America. Buffalo, New York. After miracle #1 (24-24 tie at halftime), the Buffalo State Americans decided they would not be embarrassed by the Niagara X-Men Canadians. They put it into fifth gear. Scored easily. 31-24. We got the ball on our 33-yard line. They stopped us on the next three plays. They put up a giant brick wall. Three incomplete passes. 4th down and 10 from our 33. The scoreboard read: 10:52 3rd quarter. Not a big deal. Been there before. But, wait a minute. Where were we? Not Canada. USA.

BLINK!

"Timeout."

Our new rookie quarterback, Tim, ran to the sideline.

"Streak's over, Tim. We have to punt."
"I can get the first down, coach."
"Streak's over. You punt."

You punt??? He's never punted once, not even in practice!!

"I don't want to be the one who breaks the Streak."
"Streak's over, Tim. Punt!"
"Post pass to Bryce, coach. I can get it to him. Or, I'll run."
"Streak's over, Tim. Punt the damn ball!"

Tim punted. The ball went off the side of his foot. Eleven-yard punt to the 44. A Buffalo State defender returned the ball to our 11-yard line. We lost a total of 22 yards of field position.

"You stunned ass!"
"Watch it Coach."
"I was talking to myself, Mr. Referee."

Culture Shock. Like a punch to the head. Fear of being who you are. Smash. Blinked and kicked. Eleven-yard kick. Minus 22-yard outcome. A group of kids on bicycles heckled from the sid walk behind the stands. Nasty language — questioning the size and existence of our balls.

They scored on the very next play. 38-24. Goliath up by 14 points. David on the ropes. Streak dead.

It felt like a death of a close friend. No. Family. We created it. Gave it life. While it was alive, it was actually alive. I killed it. First degree murder. The Streak Killer. Tim felt like an accomplice. But he wasn't. I acted alone. No conspiracy.

There was deafening silence on the sideline. Everyone saw me blink. Too many eyewitnesses. And, too much evidence left at the crime scene. The moment of silence that followed was for two deaths. The Streak wasn't the only thing that died.

∞

VI
388

"Half of the harm that is done in this world, is due to people who want to feel important."
- T. S. Eliot

"388. Three... eighty-eight!"

Quarterbacks are expert non-verbal communicators. Like any front-line worker, they can send a clear, potent message using simple facial expressions. Simple, silent messages.

Non-verbal language is an efficient form of wireless, high-speed communication. It does not lie. Facial expression is only one of the endless forms of powerful, truthful, non-verbal communication.

∞

"388. Three... eighty-eight!"

It was a simple message. A simple, loud message from the head coach. Not just any coach. The head coach. The message communicated a decision. A big decision. A decision that would determine whether a certified miracle would occur.

The quarterback's facial expression was unmistakable — a simple silent message. Nothing complicated. Easy to interpret. Easy to understand. A reply to the decision-maker.

A football field is like any other place — workplace, playplace — where volumes of decisions are made every minute of every day and return messages are communicated to the original sender. Reciprocal communication. Back and forth, back and forth. Warp-speed wireless connecting information. Nothing very hard about any of it.

But, simplicity is often ignored. Instead, we choose to needlessly complicate everything — the actual decision and then how to interpret the response.

Decision-making is the pulse of any team — any organization. Some decisions are difficult. But, most are simple — obvious, common-sense, no-brainer decisions. If you know what you're doing and you've been doing it long enough, decisions should not be hard to make. Experience gives us enough points-of-reference to steer our decision-making compass.

The problem with simple and obvious is what's missing. The **"absence of.**" These decisions are not sexy enough; not glamorous enough. Not deep enough. Run-of-the-mill decisions don't fuel the self-importance addiction. They should, but they don't. Simple doesn't translate into important. That's why simplicity is often ignored. To feed the beast. We want more! More importance.

When we ignore simplicity and make a stupid decision, we get a **"sign.**" One sign is the "look." The facial expression of the person who hears the stupidity.

We've been interpreting non-verbal responses since we were born. From the time people stuck their faces in our cribs to this very moment, we've seen every facial expression possible. There is not one look that we haven't seen.

Not one look we can't decipher.

"Don't roll your eyes at me, buddy."

There is no facial expression we can't interpret.

"You think this is funny?"

We are expert non-verbal translators. But if we're so smart, then why do we fail? Why do we make trainwreck decisions? Why do we not see the signs that tell us we have sprayed dangerous substances all over the place?

Two reasons. Pretentious assholeism and confucktions.

∞

"388. Three... eighty-eight!"

Pretentious assholeism is a personality disorder that develops in people whose estimation of themselves grows with each decision they make. A personality disorder caused by an internal growth — self-importance. Unless it is surgically removed, the growth will keep growing and spread. Like a virus.

Prententious assholeism causes damage. Most of the damage is collateral. A small amount is actually intended. The victim becomes a "**pretentious assholeholic**," a chronic condition that blinds. The assholeholic becomes unaware that his assholeism is spreading out of control. Can't see it any more. Or maybe does and chooses to ignore it.

The collateral damage is not limited to the external world. Internal damage is included. Left unchecked, pretentious assholeism leads to confucktions, a mysterious ailment that plagues rational thinking. Confucktions interrupt functional behaviour, leading to wide-ranging dysfunctionalism. Confucktions, like pretentious assholeism, are caused by self-importance. There are many more causes. And there are residual effects. Finding a cure is not easy. A lot of work has been done, but much more work is needed. Until a definite cure is found, beware of the "confucktionator." The multiple-confucktion monster who causes massive collateral damage.

"388!"

Prententious assholeism and confucktions are not mutually exclusive. They interact within a complex web. One breeds the other and then feeds it. With anabolic agents that produce deadly side-effects. Until a cycle grows so big that a Goliath-sized brick wall is built.

Simple, obvious, no-brainer decisions should come with a Surgeon General's warning:

"Pretentious assholeism may kill you. Second-hand pretentious assholeism may kill those around you."

If something is missing, and simple decisions are not sexy enough, not glamorous enough, not deep enough, let someone else make the simple decision.

The universe has one solution for pretentious assholeism — the reply. That silent message that boomerangs back to the sender. Every stupid decision has a reply button attached to it. The reply whizzes back at warp-speed. In bold letters, the simple silent message informs us we have made a stupid decision that needs correcting. But the problem is confucktion blocking.

Confucktions get in the way of seeing and interpreting the reply. Confucktions are sensory blockers. Blocks vision, blocks hearing, blocks thinking. Confucktions are great blockers. Football has pass blocking and run blocking. If the Niagara X-Men could block like confucktions, Goliath would have been knocked out five weeks ago. Out for the count.

Good news! One hopeful cure for both pretentious assholeism and confucktions is the intervention. Interventions don't have to be complex. They can be simple. One person or several. The key is honesty. Honesty out — honesty in.

∞

The best way to describe the quarterback's facial expression: blank stare. Frozen. Slight eye squinting. Placid face. Just like a hanging victim. Same look as the onset of heartburn. Indigestion. Ate something awful.

And direct eye contact with the original messenger. A momentary message stare-down. Two message-slingers in an alley. Face-to-face. Ready to draw. Someone has to blink.

The quarterback's simple, silent message was clear.

"Have you lost your mind?! I know your decision is stupid. Everyone knows your decision is stupid. So do you. Gotta change it."

That's part 1. Here's part 2:

"Look, I'll give you some advice. Free consultation. Either you change your thinking or I'll do it for you. I'll change it. I can do it without any mess. Like a sweeper team. No one will know what really happened. I'll fix your skewed logic like Harvey Keitel did as the cleaner in Pulp Fiction."

That's part 2. Here's part 3:

"Time's running out. Your stupid decision will affect a lot of people. I know that you know you blinked. You were incapable of common sense or rational thinking and you've made a ludicrous decision because of shock – Culture Shock. You blinked. I'll keep it a secret, but you only have one last chance to fix it."

∞

That three-part message was the only possible interpretation for the quarterback's facial expression. No ambiguity. No what-ifs. And the look stayed on message. No wavering. The return message from the quarterback stayed on track. The guy who had pressed "**send**" could simply press "**erase**" to cancel the decision and change the whole mess. But no. The decision-maker has to waste time. Do it the hard way instead. Pretend it's not happening. The sender has to avoid reality. Pretend that the decision is not being questioned. Has to pretend that the reply — the simple, silent message — may mean something else. Has to procrastinate and rationalize.

Didn't he hear me?

Of course he did. The quarterback heard me yelling the play to him. Positively. None of our quarterbacks ever had trouble hearing me yell a play from the sideline. No matter where the ball was spotted. No matter how far away from the sideline.

Vocal chords working, volume working, everything working. Does he have a bad attitude?

Of course not. He has the best attitude a coach could ask for. No bad attitude before. Why would it start now?

Is he stupid? He doesn't know what 388 means after all this time?

Of course not. He did translate it accurately. That was the problem. He knew exactly what the decision meant.

So what's his problem? What's with that look on his face?

Honesty out — honesty in. That's what the Code of Conduct said. That's the expectation.

"Just don't lie. You miss practice? Tell the truth. You miss working out? Tell the truth. You screw up? Tell the truth. No excuses. Be honest."

Honesty out — honesty in. And vice-versa. You get back what you send out.

"388!"

Like a boomerang. It comes back. Right at you. You have to be ready to catch it or it'll knock you down. Pay attention. Be careful. Get in a proper stance. Be ready to absorb the impact.

The boomerang effect worked in full force. The quarterback's confused look — that simple, silent message — was not the result of an audio problem or an attitude problem or an intelligence problem. There was another reason for the look.

Shock. Culture Shock.

∞

Coaches are obsessed with calling plays instead of letting the quarterback do it. In the 1950s and 60s, quarterbacks generally called their own plays. Coaches taught them a system and how to make decisions. Just like how parents teach their kids.

"Now that you're sixteen Wally, it's time I teach you to drive the car. Here, lemme show you. You sit in the passenger seat. I'll drive. Watch carefully and learn."

Eventually, Wally gets to sit in the driver's seat while June sits next to him in the passenger's seat. Wally practices driving with June sitting right next to him. They do this over and over until Wally gets it. After the driving instruction is done, June gives Wally the keys to the car and Wally drives on his own. To pick up friends. Girlfriends. But without his mother.

Play-calling is like teaching your children to drive. Show them. Teach the system. Then, let them practice while you stand next to them during the practice. Eventually, you have to give them the keys to the car. If you want a warp-speed no-huddle, the quarterback eventually has to be the driver. But, a balance is needed. Don't let them drive without enough experience because they'll smash the car and themselves to pieces. When they become competent, well, it's pretty emba rassing having your mother drive you around.

Modern-day coaches have become micro-managers with major trust issues. They don't give up the keys to the car. And, if they do, they grab the steering wheel at every turn. Clutch and grab all the way from the passenger side. Fighting with the quarterback to drive the car that is in the capable hands of a trained new driver. Coaches can't keep their hands off the wheel.

"388!"

Coaches believe that calling plays is the equivalent of sending people to Mars and returning them safely back to Earth.

"The next rule in Coaching 101. Call your own plays. It's too important. You're smarter than the players. You can't let anyone do this. It's too hard."

Play-calling is an obsession.

"... short pass... off-tackle... shorter pass... off-tackle again..."

The explosive growth of Madden football video games and fantasy football leagues is compelling evidence that calling plays is a deep need. Too deep. So deep that it clouds judgment.

"388!"

Why? What causes micro-managing? When the driver is fully trained, why push the driver aside and take over the steering?

"388!"

Searching for meaning, plus two addictions: approval and adrenaline. That's why. Calling the right play will hopefully bring meaning to a meaningless existence.

"Please, please let this deep pass that I just called work to reverse the dread of monotony in my life!"

Doing the same thing every day?

"Ya, but I can call football plays."

Bored out of your mind?

"No problem. I sure can call football plays."

Dreaming of escape from pointless conversations? Compensate — call football plays. Make the same decisions that you've trained your quarterback to make.

Suffering from approval withdrawal by being disconnected from planet Earth because you've spent yet another day with your face stuck to your Crackberry reading ludicrous e-mails?

Adrenaline gland shut off and stuck in the off position? Clutching your gut, guttural screams from adrenaline withdrawal?

"388!"

Magically, calling a football play cures all evils. Instant meaning. Approval fix. Adrenaline fix.

"Great call, coach! You're a genius!"

∞

After the monumental decision about what the next play will be, that decision must be protected at all costs. Top secret. Confidential. For eyes only. Except one problem. Somehow you have to let your offense know your decision.

The football micro-managing communication path is very simple. From the coach on the sideline to the quarterback on the field to the other 10 offensive players. "Sending in" the call from the sideline to the quarterback is generally the product of a military-like covert operation. The pros use technology — the quarterback's helmet is wired for sound. If a coach doesn't wear a headset, he usually suffers the wrath of fans and the media.

"HE DOESN'T WEAR A HEADSET! WHAT KIND OF COACH IS HE?"

This sort of nonsense can be heard on radio talk shows all over North America. As if wearing a headset will cure cancer, solve world hunger, correct a recession. We are led to believe that coaches have to be equipped with state-of-the-art technological communication equipment to decide to **"throw to that guy over there"** or **"hand off the ball to this guy over here."**

Without technology, there are two alternatives:

1. Shuttle. Tell a player, on the sidelines, the play. He runs to the huddle, relays the play to the quarterback and replaces a player who then comes off the field. A human information shuttle system.
2. Hand signals. The messenger, on the sidelines, uses his hands and a wide range of physical contortions to display signals that must be translated by the quarterback on the field. Part 2 of this system — to prevent the opponent from deciphering the signals, a second or third person stands next to the real messenger, sending false signals. Similar to the classic Three Stooges smack-down, minus the slaps on the back of the head.

All of this is time consuming and distracting to the quarterback.

"Did he call for a deep pass or is he just pissed off at the refs?"

If the quarterback believes the coach is pissed off, he has to remember the signal for "**HUH**?" And if the coach really is pissed off, the "**HUH**?" signal likely pisses him off more.

Often, the hand signals are downright dangerous to the quarterback. Many of us have never played quarte back, so it's easy to forget one simple fact about the job — the quarterback is the target of many hostile, mobile, and agile defensive players. On every pass play, a number of strong weight-lifters with blazing speed, sprint like madmen at the quarterback as if he just stole money from their mothers. Sometimes, these hostiles hit the quarterback. Sometimes they don't. Either way, it's stressful to have nasty muscular people chase you 50 times a game. You can't blame a quarte back if he'd like to think for himself.

Eliminate the communication from the sideline. Who would criticize a quarterback if he misinterpreted the physical gyrations because he was trying to clear his head from the pressure of being the human target of a hunting party?

Then there's the matter of communicating the play to the rest of the offense.

"Whatever you do, call the play quietly in the huddle. Don't let the defense hear."
"Don't underestimate the defense, boys... They will figure out the play."

How? How exactly will the defense figure it out? How smart are these defensive people? Are they like the guy in Good Will Hunting who wrote all those math equations on the wall in just a few seconds? Is John Nash from A Beautiful Mind playing middle linebacker? Is Jarod at strong safety?

Football is a Pavlovian laboratory — players are told the same thing over and over to the point where they believe anything.

"Huddle 10 yards from the ball! Don't get too close to the defense when you call the play!"
"Lower your voice in the huddle, son. Y'all want the whole stadium to hear the play?"

The huddle is conventional. Part of the football gospels. It evokes a lot of screaming at practice. An attempt to reverse the inevitable bad habits that the huddle promotes.

"Run back to the huddle doggonitt! What the hell are you doing walking to the huddle? This is football! This is the sloppiest huddle I've ever seen, dadgummit!! Here, lemme show y'all. Stand in a line... come on now... make a straight line!!!"

"Don't walk from the huddle! You gotta run from the huddle! Y'all have to run to the line! LET'S DO IT AGAIN UNTIL WE GET THAT HUDDLE RIGHT!"

Hours spent coercing young men to stand in a nice, neat circle and mind their manners.

The huddle is the football equivalent of a covert CIA operation. The quarterback whispers a play to his teammates who are huddled together like sheep. Conventional plays with strange names. Long, disjointed sentences whispered by the quarterback. Then, all 11 guys (including the QB) are required to accurately recall the information within a few seconds before the play starts.

"Gee Wally, keep it down! The defense will hear! You heard what coach said. Come on now."

The huddle has to be at an appropriate distance from the defense to maintain the top secrecy of the operation. The center usually has the onus of being the marker. This poor kid has to post himself at about 10 yards from where the ball is spotted, turn his back to the ball, raise his hands in the air, and scream at the top of his lungs,

"HUDDLLLLLLLLLLLE!"

When the center executes this job properly, coaches turn to each other and say:

"Now that's real leadership. Billy's a real leader out there."

The center's parents beam with pride.

"Look, Madge... Look at how he forms the huddle... He's gonna be President some day!"

In all likelihood, the center is probably frustrated beyond belief, screaming profanities at his teammates to lineup properly so he doesn't get hollered at by the coach.

Huddles are also a means of recovery. Both the offense and the defense get a chance to catch their breath. It's like the conventional strength training workout where you do one set, put the bar down for a while, sit around, wait, do another set.

There's a problem with all of this. Boredom and lethargy set in. Players straggle to and from the huddle. In the huddle, they screw around.

"Did you see that hot cheerleader second from the left?"
"Hey, that's my sister. Want a shot in the mouth?"

The conventional way of playing football. Eleven players huddle. The QB talks. They leave the huddle and line up at the ball. The QB starts calling the "**cadence**" — language to get the ball snapped in order to start the play. A typical football play is a 4-6 second burst of collective energy. Then everyone stops, relaxes, walks back to the huddle, and it starts all over again — beginning with the play-caller.

The coach's need to be a play-caller is intimately tied to the conventional "**playbook.**" A football playbook is the brain trust of all football teams. It is a team's strategic nerve centre. The conventional playbook is a huge binder. Countless pages. Each page has diagrams of plays. In slang terms, plays are called "**Xs and Os,**" referring to the symbols used for offensive and defensive players.

"Here, son, memorize this whole binder before next practice. It's your playbook."
"All 1,000 pages?"
"Yup. The diagrams and the names of each play… by the end of the week."

Then, the comparisons. Playbook envy.

"Our playbook is bigger than yours!"

∞

The Niagara X-Men use a wireless communication system for play-calling — yelling. No microphone. No headset in the quarterback's helmet. We yell the play out loud from the bench to the quarterback.

"That's pretty sneaky. You yell a phony play to fool the other team, EH?"
"That is the real play, Mr. Referee."

Up to 1993, we used conventional communication systems. To be the same as everybody else. Just in case the neighbors were watching.

We tried hand signals.

"Coach, is that a 3 or does your lower back hurt again??"
"It's a three... IT'S A THREE!"

We tried wristbands.

"3... 8... What's that last number? I can't read that small without my glasses."
"TWEEEET!... Delay of game... 15 yards."

We tried the human shuttle system — one player running onto the field, one player running off. One in. One out. Pretty basic.

"TWEEEET!... Too many men on the field... 15 yards."

We were the other team's best defensive strategy for slowing down our warp-speed no-huddle. We didn't just slow it down, we brought it to crawl. Instead of a sleek race car, we pushed a jalopy. A solution was needed. Yelling. Yelling the play from the sidelines. The fastest, cheapest, clearest, most efficient way to communicate. Our entire team hears it. Their entire team hears it. Sometimes, a new quarterback would stare, wondering if he should yell the same play again.

"Should I call the same play you just yelled?"
"Can't hurt. Just in case."

∞

"388!"

This call was not confusing to the quarterback. His confused look had nothing to do with the volume of the yelling or the translation of the yelling. Just the opposite. He knew what 388 meant.

That's why it put him in shock.

This quarterback had an excellent driving record in Canada. Called his own plays for three games. No accidents. Speeding, but no collisions. How did he do it? By calling the obvious — pass plays. Lots of them.

Over and over. From his favourite driver's seat — the shotgun. That's the quarterback's best driver's seat when he has to pass a lot. It's not crowded. Four yards behind the football as opposed to crouched down with his hands under the center's ass. The shotgun is by far, the most comfortable driver's seat. More elbow room, better view, and safety equipment better than an air bag — distance between the quarterback and the hunters.

"Here's the game plan. You call your own plays. Just like you practice. Pass a lot. Just like in practice. No-huddle. Warp-speed. Just like in practice. Stay in the shotgun. Just like in practice."

Lots and lots of passing. That's how we practice. That's how we play. Train like you fight — fight like you train.

Undefeated for three games. Combined score of 117-14. In Canada. The quarterback drove the machine just fine. But, can he drive in the USA? Does he need an American license?

"388!"

∞

The shocked look was a sign. Just like it says in the Celestine Prophesy. We get signs every day. No coincidences. All we have to do is be aware. Recognize the sign. Interpret it. Then, do something about it. And, when we are oblivious to signs, there will be more signs. Bigger signs. Sometimes with industrial strength voltage. Giant neon lights telling us what to do.

Our new rookie quarterback was very polite. No attitude. No arrogance. But, sometimes that could be a problem. Good quarterbacks are the Freudian super-ego judge of a coach's decisions. The arbiter of a coach's decision-making. The private advisor who lets you know if your decision is bad. They judge the rationality of plays called by coaches who insist on driving the same car that they taught the quarterback to drive. Good quarterbacks can politely change the play, correcting a stupid call, without pissing off the coach. Great quarterbacks can change the play, succeed, and make it look like the coach was responsible for the genius decision.

"Timeout... Coach, you were probably busy on the sideline and didn't see that the defense is using man coverage on every single play

since the first quarter. Here's an idea. How about we try a double-post on the wide-side, just like you say repeatedly during practice?"

After it works, really smart quarterbacks sprint past the bench and yell,

"Great call, coach!"

Other times, good quarterbacks invent procedures. Like tapping their helmet furiously. Followed by waving of the hands. Followed by a completely different call than the one that was sent in.

"Hey, what did that mean?"
"That was the 'request to change the call' signal, coach."
"What? When did we put in a 'change the call' signal?"
"Three weeks ago. You were probably busy and forgot."

Then there's the fake "**hang-on-a-second, things-are-really-busy-on-the-field-right-now**" look a quarterback gives you, after you send in a stupid play, followed by the quarterback sneaking up to the line and calling the right play.

"Sorry, Coach. Things got busy out there. Couldn't hear you yelling. But, you were probably going to call the same play, right?"
"Of course."

∞

The 1986 **Jeff Benoit wild celebration** not only started the "**No-kicking Streak,**" it was the tipping point. It was the catalyst for more radical change. It transformed the way we did everything. The way we taught, the way we learned, the way we performed. A paradigm shift through elimination. Addition through subtraction.

No playbook.
No signals.
No huddle.
No trick plays.
No secrecy.
No conventional thinking.
No fear of criticism.
Eventually, no Canadian games.

Jeff's team epitomized the "**reality of limitations**." Only 25 players. That's less than half the normal size of a high school roster. No junior varsity team to develop the senior varsity players. No in-house faculty to coach the team. An outsider head coach — a cop — not a teacher. That didn't go over well with high school teachers. Doesn't sit well with the football disciples. According to football gospel, only high school teachers can coach high school football. No trespassers allowed.

But, Jeff's team had pulled off a miracle the year before, in 1985. The first undefeated 10-0 season in school history. With only 25 players. The secret formula had been discovered. The weight room. Football games are not won on game day. They are won in the off-season, in the gym — lifting weights. Strength training tilts the playing field. Bigger, faster, stronger and, more important, stronger character. Sustained, intense strength training dramatically transforms high school students. It not only makes them better athletes, it develops myriad deep-rooted positive habits.

Anima Sana in Corpore Sano — sound mind in sound body… ASICS.

Strength training replaces bad habits. It is one of the best proactive strategies in the world to prevent teenagers from doing destructive things. Six grueling workouts per week engenders incredible natural growth — mentally and physically. During teenage years, natural growth is rapid. A steep incline on the muscle charts, in comparison to later in life, where gains flat-line.

High school athletes who are committed to intense, consistent strength training are not prone to self-destructive behaviour. They think twice before they get wasted on alcohol and drugs. Wasting weeks of gut-wrenching workouts. They are not stupid. Kids will not give up their investment easily.

Radical change. Working out and downsizing.

First, the playbook was eliminated. No more playbook — for offense and defense.

"No playbook?! How can any decent red-blooded team have no playbook?"

Don't need one. Replaced it with the SWAT system (Speed With Attitude Team). The system is based on a combination of police language and incredibly simple decision-making models. Memorization is replaced by strategizing and improvising. Good old-fashioned thinking. Conventional play jargon is replaced by literally saying the equivalent, *"you go here, you go there."* Clarity. Simplicity. And limitless — unlimited plays. Taught and learned in 1-2 practices. No more binders. No more paper. We went green long before Al Gore exposed us to the Inconvenient Truth.

Then, we changed the driver's seat. From the awkward crouching under the center's ass seat to the shotgun. A luxury driver's seat.

The signals were the next thing on the chopping block. Replaced it with good old-fashioned yelling. Yelling the play from the bench to the quarterback. A temporary communication path that was used only for as long as the quarterback was learning to drive. Then, he called his own plays. The QB became the yeller. He yelled the actual play, out loud, to his teammates, with the defense listening.

To simplify even more, the quarterback actually looks directly at each of his receivers and tells them what to do — in police talk. The police language. Short, simple, to the point.

On a bad day, our quarterbacks pass for 300 yards. On a good day — 600. On a crazy day — 836 yards and 8 touchdowns. That performance got a quarterback featured in *Sports Illustrated*.

The warp-speed **"no-huddle"** approach doubled everything. The volume of practice reps, the number of plays in a game, players' experience, players' development, and especially, opponents' fatigue. Warp-speed makes football into a fitness contest — physically and mentally. It becomes a race to see who weakens first. Everything speeds up. Thinking, decision-making, breathing, lactic acid buildup.

All trick plays were cut from the system. Not one left. Trick plays represent the height of strategic deception. Fake to this guy, lateral to that guy who passes to him over there. This complexity needs significant practice. Time that we can't afford. What you focus on grows. So we focused on passing.

"When you yell the play from the sideline, you're not actually yelling the real play, right?"

Even when you eliminate secrecy and yell the truth out loud, the opposing coaches believe you are trying to deceive them. No one believes that the truth is being yelled out loud. Double-deception. When you tell the truth and people don't believe it because they are accustomed to and expecting lies, they won't believe the truth. They believe the truth is a lie.

The only problem with the strategy of yelling plays is convincing rookies.

"But won't the other team hear the play, coach?"

Rookie players are the product of conventional thinking. They have been conditioned to believe that the defense is made up of expert CIA analysts. Like the Enigma code-breakers. Luckily, conformity is not terminal in student-athletes. One simple explanation cures them.

"Listen, son, here's why we yell the play out loud. First, we use the police language. No other team on the planet uses it. Secondly, our own defense has a hard time figuring it out after weeks of practice, so how can their defense figure it out in a few seconds? And one more thing... if we are good enough, we should be able to line up on offense and tell the defense exactly what we're going to do and then do it!"

Motivation 101. Everyone roars with approval.

"Ya, that's right. We're badasses! It don't matter if they hear the play!"

After this works in practice and then in games, our players start believing they can beat the New England Patriots.

"Hey, coach, this is what Peyton Manning does. He points and yells the play right out loud!"
"That's right, son, you're just like Peyton Manning."

Motivation 201. Simplicity builds off-the-chart confidence. Show them it works — instant buy-in. Then, let them do it. Long-term buy-in. Unshakable belief. That's why we let quarterbacks call their own plays. No micro-managing.

∞

"388!"

A simple three-digit number communicated the final call — a running play, not a pass play. A running play where the quarterback has to change driver's seat — from the luxury car shotgun seat to the cramped crouched-down-with-hands-under-the-center's-ass driver's seat.

Three simple numbers. The first number communicated who will be the ballcarrier. The second number told him where to run. The third number told him how he will get the ball and also told the blockers who to block — the type of running play. In this case, the "**type**" was the ancient freeze option running play that was kept in the attic of the SWAT system. We dusted it off. Let's trick Goliath.

The rookie quarterback turned and walked to the line of scrimmage.

You want 388? 388 it is. You drive.

Didn't the quarterback recognize the symptoms — that the head coach had been exposed to the gamma rays of Culture Shock?

Change the damn play! Salvage dignity! Restore common sense! Just take the car keys!

But, Culture Shock must be contagious. The quarterback did not change the call. For the first time in recent memory, he positioned himself in a foreign place — crouched down under the center's ass instead of in the shotgun formation, and started the cadence. He barked out the play for everyone to hear.

"388!"

Now the rest of the team knew — Culture Shock had set in. The virus had spread. Instantly. To the other 10 players on the field. Simple, silent messages — times 10.

∞

VII
Natural Selection

"In the struggle for survival, the fittest win out at the expense of their rivals because they succeed in adapting themselves best to their environment."

- **Charles Darwin**

"Check!"

A one-word solution. After he relayed the 388 to the other 10 players on the field, all the quarterback had to say was "**check**" before he continued. "**Check**" means, *"cancel everything I just said. I'm changing my mind. Here's the new play."*

"**Check**" is the official transfer of the car keys. The quarterback climbs into the driver's seat. Check is not only simple efficient communication, it's one of the official antidotes for Culture Shock. A syringe filled with the substance that counteracts a confucktion. One shot of "**check**" and all is well again.

"Listen, use check any time... ANY TIME something goes wrong. You go brain-dead and don't remember what you just called? Yell check. I go brain-dead and call a stupid play, yell check. Easy. Right?"
"Got it, coach."

At practice, quarterbacks screw up on purpose just so they can yell "**check**." Makes them sound cool. Makes them feel in charge. Empowered. The rest of the players think they can apply for the Mensa Club because they translated "**check**" properly. All of them start believing they have NFL-level IQ.

"Man, the QB checked off a lot today!"

But, instead of injecting the antidote, the quarterback simply continued the cadence. The cadence tells the quarterback's teammates what the play will be — the play, their assignments, and when the ball will be snapped to start the play. The cadence is the quarterback's turn to yell what sounds like nonsensical language.

The Niagara X-Men cadence is unique. The quarterback yells a total of three plays. One is the real play. Two are called "**dummy plays.**" Not real. Only one is live. The other two are bullshit. The quarterback has a sneaky way of informing his teammates which play is real. He either tells them at the beginning of the drive, for example, "**three plays called, first play is live,**" or he yells a number before each play that communicates the total number of plays and which one is live. Either way, 33% of the cadence is the truth and 67% is nonsense.

In this case, either of the two bullshit plays would have been better than the real play.

"388!"

∞

Waiting for the ball to be snapped to start the play can be either boring or exciting. It depends on the situation. In this case, there was a sense of anticipation. As anticipation heightens, the senses sharpen.

Fight or flight.

Suddenly, there was a moment of clarity. Time slowed down. Four observations became crystal clear:

1. Our offensive line was crooked.
2. There was no discernible muscularity on our offensive line.
3. Their outside linebacker was muscular.
4. Their muscular outside linebacker would be unblocked, i.e., he had a clear path to the quarterback.

One explanation for all the above: Canadian football culture FTA. The "**fail to appear**" syndrome.

"**FTA**" is a Criminal Code offence committed by criminals who don't show up for their day in court. Ideally, the phrase "**fail to appear**" should be used only in the Criminal Justice System, not in relation to football. Sadly, it applies to football.

A number of Canadian players have a strong tendency to fail to appear in three places:

1. Weight room.
2. Practices.
3. Games.

Football FTA is a cultural phenomenon. Athletes want to play a violent sport but they don't want to prepare for it. Athletes want scholarships to American universities but they don't want to pay the price. Football FTA symbolizes a social and psychological crisis that developed in the latter part of the 20th century. It exploded in the 21st century.

"I've never heard of such a thing!"

… as expressed by a coach from the football-mad state of Michigan. He was shocked — Culture Shocked.

"You mean they miss games?!"
"Correct. They simply don't show up. They tell no one. Complete surprise."
"That makes no sense. Why would someone do that?"
"Some of the reasons include, 'I had to go to Thanksgiving supper,' 'I slept in,' 'I thought the game was tomorrow.'"
"That's a nightmare!"

It is. Our reality is a nightmare. A nightmare with two types of monsters. Goliath on the one side and FTAs on the other.

"Hey, David. Are you going to slingshot practice today?"
"Na, I have to Twitter."

A nightmare is fiction. Or, friction. But, it's not reality. There's a problem when reality is stranger than fiction.

"Hey, Goliath. Where's that kid? He's not here?"
"Looks like he failed to appear. Let's go home."

∞

"Scholarship. More muscle. Less fat."

The Niagara X-Men trilogy. The three most common answers to the question, *"What are your goals?"*

None of these goals happen randomly. Nothing just happens. These goals all require tests. A test is any obstacle that forces the athlete to:

1. **Struggle**: stress the body to make it grow stronger.
2. **Survive**: stress the mind to make it grow stronger.

95

Athletic tests must force a decision — continue or quit. Stay or leave. Every workout, every practice must be a test or it is only a maintenance exercise.

No test, no growth. These goals are connected. The strength of one depends on the strength of the others. The cycle of strength. The strongest athletes keep climbing. Climbing ladders.

The path to getting stronger is a road full of tests. Game day is not the big test. It's contest day. It's the by-product of many big tests but it is not the biggest. How you get there is the big test, not what you do when you get there. What happens on game day is a manifestation of the training. The road. It shows exactly how you got there. The contest is a summary of the training. A training narrative.

"What kind of workouts do they do?"

Watch the game. Watch the contest. You'll see every set, every rep of the training.

It is impossible to perform at a higher level than you prepare for.

∞

Struggle + Survival = Strength

Gawking + Walking = Strolling

A real test fits the first formula. It includes the two elements of struggle and survival that produce one outcome: strength. If one element is missing, it's not a test. It's tourism. Tourism is the opposite of a test. No struggle, no survival, no strength. Tests involve first-string players. Tourists are not on the roster. First-string players play because they passed the test. Tourists never took the test. Instead of struggle + survival, tourists stroll. Gawk and walk.

The strength of the test determines exactly how strong the competitor becomes. The game day opponent has to be strong. The contest opponent has to provide a struggle. But the most important struggle has to happen before the contest. Every workout is a game. Every practice is a competition. And, the score has to be kept during every practice and every workout. No exceptions. Each workout has to be a test. A separate bona fide test. As they add up, the road tests have to be bigger than the contest game-day test. Way bigger.

Struggle to survive — survive to struggle. When the road becomes the meaning, the tourist becomes a player. A real athlete lives for the struggle.

∞

The **KEISS** to success: **K**nowledge, **E**xecution, **I**ntensity, **S**truggle, **S**urvival.

Learn what to do. Find a coach — a mentor.

You can't learn more than your mentor teaches you? Find a smarter mentor.

Do what you learn. Do it against the strongest opponent.

Climb a ladder. If you fall, get up.

Doing what you learn requires reps. Countless hours of repetitions. But, all reps are not created equal. There are three classifications of reps. Ordinary reps. Extraordinary reps. Mediocre reps. The type of rep corresponds with the type of athlete we become — and the type of game we play. Ordinary, extraordinary, or mediocre.

Weak opponents won't put up a struggle. Find a Goliath. Only a Goliath makes a David. The bigger the struggle, the steeper the climb. The climb teaches survival — how to get off the canvas. Again and again, and again.

∞

You have to fight Goliath many times before the contest to beat Goliath on game day. No one can beat Goliath without beating him before. That means you have to build an opponent that resembles Goliath. Simulated Goliaths. Simulations prevent demolitions.

You can build two giant opponents during every workout and every practice. They are connected. Two for the price of one. Plus, you can decide how big and scary you want them to be. You can decide when to stop the fight. You can even decide whether to fight at all. The choices are all yours.

The first opponent does not have to be human. It can be a bar and metal plates to lift. It can be a road to sprint. All you need are dirty clothes. You can customize this opponent so that you can't complain about it later. Strong or weak, you are the decision-maker. Fight whoever you want.Make the bar heavier or lighter. Lengthen or shorten the run. There is no map. No blueprint. You create the opponent.

The second opponent is not visible but it's your closest partner. Your brain. Your mind. It's the real Goliath. Even tougher than the real thing. This opponent is the meanest sonofabitch you'll ever meet. A cruel, viscous bastard. Cold-hearted, Novocaine-in-the-blood monster. It won't stop. It's indefatigable. Jacked up on steroids, caffeine, and high-grade B-12. Keeps coming. Round after round. No rest period. No bell. Tries to knock the shit right out of you by trying to make you quit.

It throws punches, powerful right- and left-handed rocket launchers, non-stop from every angle — front, side, even the illegal kind from behind. Kicks you when you're down. Uses every weapon it can find — fear, self-doubt, scare tactics. It's an artist. It can create graphic visions of hell. The 9th layer of hell. When it wins, it goes on cruise control — habitual torment that leads not only to chronic quitting, it stops you from ever climbing into the ring again.

When the mind wins, you won't even walk into the arena, let alone the ring.

The good news is that you can beat the piss out of your internal monster if the first opponent is big enough. If you build a monster training opponent (human or non-human), you can kill the monster in the mind.

The bad news is that you can't beat any Goliath by failing to appear.

∞

When the external opponent is strong enough to pound the shit out of the internal beast, the threshold has been crossed. The strongest survived.

Muscle is built. Fat is lost. Scholarships are earned.

But the threshold can't be crossed without taking the road leading to it.

The key to crossing the threshold is developing the skill of "**no-option**" decisions. The good news is that it requires only a two step process and anyone can do it:

1. Decide on an "**outside the box**" challenge. Decide on doing something that is positioned outside your comfort zone, at that moment in time. Not the past, not the future; at that moment.
2. Eliminate all options except one. That's the key. Eliminate all the negative alternatives — those created by the rationalization that lead to quitting. Rationalization includes excuses, denial, blaming. Keep only one choice — the positive choice. The reason that keeps you in the ring. This reduces decision-making to a non-decision. Habitual "**no-brainers**." By definition, it is no longer a decision. It becomes second-nature to do what has to be done.

∞

American high school football is a testing ground for the "**Natural Selection**" process. Survival of the fittest. The environment is intense enough to force a decision — get stronger and move up to the next level or stay weak and move out.

Football is not just part of the American culture, it *is* their culture. The bar is set high. The strongest possible competition is expected.

The strength of your opponent determines your strength.

Those who compete, adapt. Adaptation slingshots the athlete to the next level. High school football becomes a change agent. It not only provides a centre stage to perform on, but also a grueling stage that separates the strong from the weak. A filter system. A stage that will not allow the weak to survive. The weak are separated. The fittest survive and move on to university.

The phenomenal amount of money invested in American high school football sends a powerful message to athletes and coaches, "we take it seriously so you have to take it seriously." That's why American high schools have stadiums. Sold-out stadiums.

In Canada, we don't have sold-out high school stadiums — or high school stadiums at all. That sends a message also. A powerful message but an opposite one, "we don't take it seriously, so you don't have to take it seriously either." As a matter of fact, we don't give a shit so you don't have to give a shit either. You don't even have to show up.

FTA — cause and effect.

Canadian high school football is a recreational activity in comparison with American high school football. It is not a natural selection process. Why?

No mandatory year-round strength training under the supervision of a strength coach.

No August two-a-day practices. No two-a-days period. Not even in September.

Wednesday Afternoon Sunlight versus Friday Night Lights.

Next-of-kin attendance versus packed stadiums.

In a United States high school, if you don't workout in the weight room, you will not play, or you will not succeed, and you will never be recruited by a university. Football is a high-risk sport. The weight room is a major part of high-risk training. It builds body armour. The natural equipment needed to protect an athlete from the effects of brutal collisions. It builds the physical and mental strength to be a force and deliver force.

Canadian high schools do not have an authentic weight room culture. The gym is not part of the "**high school experience.**" A small number of high school players are dedicated to intense, structured strength training and conditioning. Those programs with a strength coach, who insists on structured weight training, dominate. The weight room is the place where programs are built.

American high school pre-season starts in early August with two practices per day. Their regular season and post-season may include 12-14 games deep into November.

Canadian high school pre-season generally starts on the first day after Labour day. Often, the season is a total of 6-7 games. If you count reps only, American high school players get more playing experience in their pre-season than Canadian kids get in their entire season. Factor in the regular-season and post-season, and an American high school career provides more than double the playing experience of a Canadian high school player.

All of this amounts to Canadian high school football players being out-of-touch with reality regarding United States scholarships. Delusional.

A typical Canadian player has no idea what it takes to get a full scholarship to an American university. Including academics.

Those Canadians who do advance to American universities suffer extreme Culture Shock. The physical/mental condition of a Canadian high school graduate and the intensity of an American university pre-season practice are incompatible. They don't mix. Canadian high school football players are generally not the product of natural selection. There is no separation of the weak from the strong. In fact, the environment causes the weak to falsely believe they are strong. In the words of an esteemed Big Ten NCAA strength coach, who has coached a number of Canadian high school players, *"Soft. Nice kids, but soft. Physically and mentally."*

This certainly does not apply to every Canadian high school kid. Some are trailblazers.

Jeff Benoit, who started the No-kicking Streak, was part of a transformation that opened doors to American universities for Canadian high school players. Jeff was one of two Canadian running backs who played together, in the same backfield, at Mansfield University — an NCAA university in the renowned Pennsylvania State Athletic Conference. PSAC has produced a number of NFL players, including Andre Reed of the Buffalo Bills.

Two Canadian running backs starting on one team. In the early 1990s. Culture Shock. The other running back was Dean Stewart from Toronto. Dean destroyed records. Jeff earned All-American honors. Both were drafted by CFL teams. Their on-field accomplishments made news. But their weight room accomplishments became legendary. Pound-for-pound, they were the strongest guys on their team. Both were indefatigable in the gym. Strong physically and mentally. Culture Shock times two.

Jeff almost never got there. We sent his game film to 68 American universities over two years. His game film showed unrivaled football performance, but nothing happened. No scholarship offers.

The best evaluation came from a famous Big Ten coach:

"I can go to a track meet in Florida and find ten players as fast as Jeff and who played against the best competition. No offense to Jeff, but he hardly got touched."

Hardly got touched.

It doesn't matter what you do, what matters is who you do it against. The level of competition matters. The strength of the opponent matters. Athletic performance is judged first by who the opponent is. Then, by who you are.

∞

"We're talking about practice, not a game... practice."

Allen Iverson can talk like this because he actually spent countless hours practicing before becoming a pro NBA star. Canadian football players need to practice. A lot. Oddly, Canadian players think practice is optional. They think it's a necessary evil — an inconvenience dreamed up by draconian coaches. For some reason, many Canadian high school players believe they have reached their peak when they become a high school star. Somehow, high school success translates into an, **"I've arrived"** belief. **"I don't need practice — I know how to play."**

The **"10-year expert"** rule has probably never been explained to most Canadian high school players. It takes a decade of dedicated, intense work and practice to become an expert at anything. Not just any type of practice. Not just any type of work. The **"natural selection"** type. Sure, there are the core old-school throwbacks who love to practice (and practice hard) but that number shrinks every year. The volume of our total missed practices is staggering. Mind-boggling. It makes it impossible to become competitive. Minimum reps versus maximum reps. No contest.

If football was as sacred as hockey, **"fail to appear"** would disappear from Canadian football. If hockey players failed to appear, the nation would revolt and mourn. A cultural apocalypse. The white rider would appear at every hockey rink in Canada. Fail to appear for a football game is not a big deal because football is not sacred. Fail to appear does not cause Culture Shock in Canada. But it does in the United States.

The reason for the FTA crisis is simple: a criminal-type of rationalization in response to cognitive dissonance. Cognitive dissonance is a horrible form of internal conflict. It generates gut-wrenching stress when one acts contrary to one's personal beliefs. Brutal guilt. As horrible as cognitive dissonance is, it is one of the most potent motivators known to mankind. It motivates humans to change by doing either a positive act or a negative act.

Committing a crime causes varying strengths of cognitive dissonance, from moderate stress to gut-wrenching guilt. When a crime is committed, there are only two ways to eliminate the horrid effects of cognitive dissonance — confession or rationalization. There are no other ways. Two diametrically opposed methods will accomplish the same thing — release guilt and change the inner conflict. Without releasing it, guilt just moves around. And around. From one body part to another. Wreaking havoc. To mind and body.

An admission of guilt, to anyone, does the trick. It gets the guilt off the chest — literally. The simple act of admitting the crime not only instantly relieves the brutal inner conflict, it is the first step toward a personal paradigm shift — rehabilitation and reintegration into society as a fully-functional person.

Rationalization also does the trick. It accomplishes the same result as confessing the crime. Rationalization is self-deception. A deep form of excuse-making and denial that results in delusional thinking. Rationalization lowers personal moral beliefs and character,to increasingly lower depths, eventually shattering the personality.

"Criminal rationalization" is an extreme form of self-deception where a person can justify to himself horrible acts by intense delusion. A calming self-dialogue intended to create a false reality.

This type of rationalization applies also to any type of athletics, including life-long fitness training. It prevents athletic peak performance. It blocks athletic self-actualization. When the sport or the training becomes too hard, cognitive dissonance develops. An uncomfortable inner conflict is the start of the internal debate — should I continue or should I quit?

Cognitive dissonance forces a decision — move forward or move away. Moving forward is the athletic equivalent of confessing to a crime. The athlete acknowledges the challenge, decides to improve, and accepts all the failures and bumpy roads.

Conversely, a decision to move away is a decision to stop. This decision emerges from rationalizing that missing a game, practice, or training is not a big deal. Instead of admitting that the challenge is too tough, the athlete makes excuses.

"I wasn't starting. I got screwed."
"I have to work. I'm a victim."

If rationalization is not corrected, habitual dysfunctional behaviour develops. There are two key points to all this:

1. Suffering from cognitive dissonance has an upside. It has the potential to motivate positive change. Inner conflict is good when it motivates positive change. When it propels us to stretch past the sticking point.
2. The starting point to suffering cognitive dissonance is our belief system. We have to have a strong understanding of right from wrong in order to have an effective starting point. Cognitive dissonance becomes a motivator.

If a high school player does not have the correct belief system about football practice, strength training, and athletic preparation in general, he can't suffer cognitive dissonance. He won't change. That's why we have to change the culture before changing the person.

But changing the culture leads to the greatest football paradox of all — the intensity of practice. How do you prepare young student-athletes to play a viscous sport? Light practices or heavy practices? Soft. Intense.

If football were invented today, the sport would be met with intense opposition — just like ultimate fighting. Two MMA fighters beating each other in a cage?

"BAN THE SPORT! TOO MUCH VIOLENCE!"

Politicians, the media. Everyone had to get their two cents in when UFC was introduced.

"Ultimate fighting is barbaric. We must ban MMA to preserve our civilized society."

Governments got involved. There weren't enough problems for them to fix. Wars, terrorism, economic disaster, social injustices, disease.

"Let's take on MMA and UFC."

People think it's crazy to have two highly-skilled, committed, fit athletes fight in a cage, but it's perfectly acceptable to have 11 guys, armed with helmets and shoulder pads, run as fast as possible at a guy holding a football, and smash him to the ground. Even though they know that some of them are unskilled and weak. Physically and mentally. Unskilled, unfit UFC fighters are not allowed in the ring. But unskilled, unfit young men are allowed to put on football equipment and beat each other up.

For that matter, how would the great Canadian pastime fare if it was created and introduced to civilized society today? How would hockey pass the social conscience test?

"Madame Speaker... I'm introducing legislation to ban this new barbarism. 12 guys wearing sharp knives attached to their boots, running around on a slippery rink, armed with wooden sticks, hacking and swinging them at each other like madmen... firing a puck at 100 mph at some guy standing in front of a net, bashing each other into solid boards... and fist-fighting in, what amounts to, a LARGE CAGE ON ICE."

Death, concussions, broken necks and knee surgeries head up the list of potential consequences that a young man may suffer while playing football. To cover our asses legally, we have to warn players, in writing, about the "**potential of catastrophic injuries.**" Catastrophic injury? That's sport? No, it's madness.

All violent contact sports are bloodbaths. There is nothing worse than the lump in your gut watching a player (yours or theirs), somebody's child, getting strapped to a stretcher. Then, driving to the emergency ward praying that you'll see him walk.

So, how do you prepare? Soft or intense? Football is a high-risk activity. It calls for high-risk training.

Train like you fight — fight like you train.

You have to simulate what you intend to do in order to do it. Practice is a simulation.

It is impossible to perform at a higher level than you prepare for.

But that means hard work. Intense, consistent hard work. The problem is that not everyone wants to commit to the grueling demands of high-risk training.

∞

Only 29 dressed for the last game — the Buffalo State game. Twenty-nine is as small a roster size as you can get. But, that number is not surprising because another 66% rule applies. Two-thirds of players will quit high-risk training. Every year, we start with over 100 Canadian high school graduates. About 66% quit. Why? Because two things are too tough — our training and our opponents. Their opponent? Their mind and their brain.

The X-Men weight room programs and practices are demanding. They have to be experienced to be believed. Those who stay improve dramatically — body, mind, and soul. Those who leave miss out on a once-in-a-lifetime opportunity to stretch themselves. The Niagara X-Men are the Navy SEALS of Canadian football. The only difference is the bell — there is no bell to ring for those who leave. However, like the SEALS, those who quit are never embarrassed — ever. Football is not for everyone. Neither is X-Men training. If a player leaves, no one says a word. Those who stay are rewarded.

Countless players quit during the pre-season no-pads, non-contact workouts called, "**Muscle Academy.**" This training is an intense one-hour weight lifting and running session. In this postmodern era, it is now fashionably called "**boot camp**" by many fitness experts. The postmodern version of Muscle Academy is considerably softer than the modern era — the 1980s and 90s where the X-Men Muscle Academy training intensity and volume were unmatched. Players quit back then, but those who stayed developed into fierce competitors.

The postmodern, softer version has coincided with the Internet era. Players spend more time on a keyboard than in a gym. They would rather play the video version of football than the real thing. Facebook is more appealing than arranging a tackle football game at the local park. MySpace, YouTube, and text-messaging has replaced the countless hours of running and jumping. Before the Internet age, you couldn't drive in any Canadian city without having to slow down for a street hockey game. Now the streets are clear.

The Cyberspace softness didn't seem to afflict American university football players. Exhibit A: Two weeks before the finale in Buffalo, the Niagara X-Men traveled to Utica University, near Syracuse New York. The X-Men played a Division III junior varsity team that was only five years old. Division III is the lowest level of American university. All are non-scholarship players. But the "lowest-level" cannot be confused with "no-level." There is really no such thing as a "lowest level" of post-secondary football in the USA. There is simply no room at the top for every player. Every level is vicious. Every level is both the product of, and a stage for, natural selection. The fit got there. The weak did not.

In the second quarter of the Utica game, the most vicious tackles imaginable were made by two Utica players on two Niagara X-Men. First, a Utica defensive back tackled one of our receivers so hard that the receiver went airborne, like on the cartoons. He laid on his back. Out for the count. Two trainers worked on him. Thankfully, he walked off the field under his own power.

Five minutes later, it got worse. Our biggest, strongest, fastest athlete (a.k.a. "**the stud**") caught a pass. He was hit by a Utica linebacker. Actually, no, he collided with him. It made the same noise as a car crash. Our best athlete lay motionless. Then, the convulsions started. Trainers worked furiously. The convulsions stopped. But, he was still out. It took forever for him to regain consciousness.

Quitter is a harsh word. Let's called it "**a decision to leave**." Those who leave football after committing to a team are "**rep-robbers**." They commit theft. They steal reps from those who are committed to the team. When a player quits, he walks away with a ton of reps. Wasted reps.

Stealing reps is a deadly type of theft. It has a profound negative effect on the entire team. Rep-robbing deprives the rightful owner of those reps the opportunity to develop. The cumulative effect is worse. The team fails to grow.

In Canada, hockey is the culture. It's the only sport that matters. Canadian kids dream of winning the Stanley Cup. Soft Canadians? The Stanley Cup is the hardest trophy to win in the world. During two months of NHL playoffs, you'll see toothless Canadian players with busted-up faces, hurling their bodies in front of slapshots to stop 100 mph pucks. Bashing each other into boards at incredible speeds. Fist-fighting and trying to beat each other's brains out for the privilege of raising a silver trophy. It's UFC on ice.

No sport allows the level of violence that the NHL permits. The NHL playoffs are the most grueling, demanding sport tournament on planet Earth. Football in Canada – not on the same frequency as hockey in Canada. It's not in the same area code as hockey. It's simply not part of the culture.

Why are Canadian hockey players the toughest athletes in pro sports? How does 21-year old Sidney Crosby become the youngest captain to hoist the Stanley Cup? How does Mario Lemieux come back from cancer to win the NHL scoring title — in the same year? The same reason why Americans are better football players. Natural selection. Both sport cultures result in survival of the fittest. Canadian amateur football culture does not.

The Colgan Institute identified two obstacles that hinder development:

1. Coddling/cossetting — defined as indulging student-athletes by permitting and enabling inappropriate, immature conduct that promotes dependency and weakness, and
2. Insufficient challenge — defined as a protection from failure, including weak competition, that does not raise the bar of expectations and fails to inject new, rigorous learning.

Find the strongest external opponent and train hard. This will strengthen our toughest opponent — our worst enemy. What's inside us.

Coaching should come with a Surgeon General's warning: *"Fail to Appear Syndrome can cause serious health issues including acedia."*

"Acedia? What's that?"

Acedia is a nasty condition that prevents happiness. St. Thomas Aquinas coined this Latin word to define a pesky mental state that gets in the way of enjoying things that are truly good. It is a spiritual paralysis that blocks the ability to look past the bad. Acedia is a sticking point. It makes us see only the bad. Impossible to see the good. One of the symptoms, according to St. Thomas Aquinas, is "to look upon something worthwhile and good as impossible to achieve whether alone or with the help of others." Left unchecked, acedia leads to deep darkness. Despair. Happily there is a cure — faith. Acedia is a sin against faith. It's brought on by perceived hopelessness. Acedia can become a culture itself. It can be both the cause and the effect of Culture Shock.

How do you change a culture? How do you become fit to survive? Guerilla Ontology is one strategy. Paul Van Riper taught another.

Guerilla Ontology is a practice that introduces people to radically new ideas. The goal is to cause cognitive dissonance. Create internal discomfort by challenging prior, rigid beliefs. The phrase "**guerilla ontology**" derives from:

1. Guerilla warfare: a strategy that combines speed, mobility and shock, used by a small weaker group to fight a larger stronger group. Mobile, agile, hostile.
2. Ontology: the study of existence — reality. Reality is self-programmed. It is a worldview produced by lived experience. Guerilla Ontology seeks to change the subject's perceived reality.

Paul Van Riper is a retired marine Lieutenant General. In 2000, the Pentagon planned a war game called "**The Millennium Challenge '02**," the largest, costliest war game in history. Blue team (good guys) versus the Red team (bad guys). Lt. General Van Riper was asked to lead the bad guys. His role? A rogue military commander who broke away from his government in the Persian Gulf, threatening to overwhelm the entire region in war. They gave him a team that had no chance of winning. The Blue team was overwhelmingly the stronger opponent — a Goliath.

The Blue team lost. Badly. Goliath got pounded. Out for the count. Van Riper used counter-culture tactics. His unconventional thinking closed the gap between his small unit and the monster Blue team.

First, he was preemptive. He struck first. He didn't sit back and wait to be attacked.

Second, he taught his team to make rapid decisions under pressure with limited information. He used the unconventional theory that real-life decisions are not the product of complex analysis but, instead, emerge from a rapid "**sizing up**" of a situation and acting on it instantly, drawing on experience and intuition. The Blue team's failure was attributed to a system that required them to stop and talk things over to figure out what to do. The Red team didn't stop. They thought on the run.

Third, he valued improvisation. Spontaneity is not random. Successful decision-making in high-risk situations can only be achieved by practicing high-risk decision-making. Training has to simulate the intended outcome. Simulation develops improvisation. Great improvisers are great performers. Van Riper didn't simply put his team on centre stage and hope they would improvise. He designed practices to train his team in improvisation. Simulations — to generate successful spontaneity. Spontaneity cannot be defended.

Fourth, he did not micro-manage. He trusted his team after they were trained properly. Those on the frontline were expected to be innovative and use initiative. Van Riper valued the experience and judgment of his team.

"You are the ones on the battlefield — you're in a better position to make decisions."

Fifth — simplicity. No overloading of information. Simplify and limit communications. Once the bullets start flying, too much information becomes a burden. No long meetings. No over-analysis. No complexity.

Van Riper's legend started in Vietnam, as commander of a marine battalion. One day, the skipper of the company radioed to notify him of heavy fighting against a much larger North Vietnamese regiment. Only nine marines against 121 North Vietnamese. Van Riper responded that he would send a reactionary force if the skipper needed one. Van Riper had faith that the company had been trained properly — capable of disrupting a stronger opponent. Put them off their tactics. He trained them. He believed in their strength.

∞

There are a number of positives about dressing only 29 players for a university football game in the USA. It's easier to remember names. Players get more playing time. Not many will be on the bench. Less equipment has to be purchased. Al Gore is happier. The climate is improved because a few mini-vans use less gas than a big highway coach bus.

Third quarter. Buffalo State was pulling away. 38-24. Seemed like a lost cause. But this time, the outcome was different. Two more drives.

First drive. 88 yards, 10 plays, 14-yard touchdown pass with 7:16 left in the fourth quarter. The two-point conversion failed. 38-30.

Final drive: 1:56 left in the game. Ball on our nine-yard line. Had to gain 91 yards. A long road. A struggle. 12 plays later, a touchdown pass with four zeros on the clock. Survival.

38-36. Natural selection. Leaving the comfort zone of Canadian football was a giant leap. The first four games exposed the gap between American and Canadian football. But, that gap closed to two points, with one play left.

∞

There was a fifth observation during the quarterback cadence for the last play — the two-point conversion play. The fifth observation was the opposing sideline. Silence. Their sideline was in deep silence. Too deep. They were in shock. Deep, Culture Shock.

The silence was gratifying. The shock was gratifying. Better than winning.

Culture Shock can be either a positive or a negative. It can weaken or it can strengthen. It can be the natural selection process needed to survive.

388, *un*checked.

∞

VIII
Monsters

"He who fights with monsters, must take care to not become a monster."
                                                    - Friedrich Nietzsche

"What do you think you're doing?"

I stared at the back plate of my parked car. So did she. The plate with "**ONTARIO**" printed on it.

"Errr... I'm here from Canada. Errr... playing your JV team. Ahem... football. Just parked for a second. Is that OK?"

Mumbling follows scolding.

She was about 60 years old. Fit. Pleasant-looking. Except for that smug look — just like those referees.

"Football?"
"Yes."
"Do you know who you're playing? Our varsity team won yesterday 49-14!"
"Yes, you have a great program."
"We're gonna kick your ass!"
"Fair enough. You want me to move the car?"
"No. I'm only ribbin' ya. I'm the registrar of the university. You know, you've been a good sport. And to show you that there's no hard feelings, after we thump you, I'm going to send you a gift. A great book called The Tipping Point."

When someone recommends a book, any book, it's a message. A sign. You're supposed to read it.

Greenville is a beautiful village in western Pennsylvania. Just like Walnut Grove in Little House on the Prairie — except for the university and the football stadium with the multi-million-dollar turf.

Turf envy. Stadium envy. Weight room envy. The trilogy of pre-game jealousies suffered by Canadian football coaches visiting the United States.

113

Thiel University was old, but their Division III football program was a monster. Ten minutes before kickoff, the earth shook — literally. Then a thunderous bang a few seconds later. All under a blue sky and shining sun. Great backdrop for a pre-game speech for our penultimate game.

"The football gods are smiling on us!"

After the game, we saw a CNN truck parked downtown Greenville, Pa, had been the epicenter of an earthquake. Real Culture Shock.

"Do you understand where you are?"

The question was rhetorical. The tight end raised his hand.

"We're in close proximity to where five hall-of-fame NFL quarterbacks played high school football, coach."

Stunned silence.

The tight end never spoke. He was the most highly-recruited player on our team. Sought after on both sides of the border. Averaged 11 receptions and 189 yards per game. Blue-chip recruit. The proverbial **"stud."** Worked out in the weight room. Lifted hard. Got strong as an ox. Fast and intense. Nasty when he carried the ball. Never missed practice. Practiced like a beast — like a monster. We threw the ball to him on the first play of every game. Deep pass every first play. To send a message: *"get used to this."* We threw to him often. Just for fun… to watch him run over people.

Ohhhh, Caaaanada.

But he never talked — ever. The unassuming, polite, quiet type.

"How'd you know that?"
"You told us after our first practice, coach."

Impressive. Six weeks ago, a post-practice #1 speech that included an impassioned history/geography lesson. A spirited intense event — a motivational speech. But, the effects of acedia had set in before the speech even ended.

"No one's listening. No one gives a shit. Why am I wasting my breath?"

Acedia. A brick wall. An obstacle, not a ladder. Acedia affects thinking. The misdirecting voice implies only the worst. It never inspires.

Got to give it credit though. The acedia-voice stays on message. Same thing over and over. Acedia owns a small key ring with only one key on it. It carries that key as it moves around in your head. The key unlocks the door with the sign, **"Caution — Bad Memories — DO NOT OPEN."** This same key keeps another door locked. The **"Good Memories"** door.

"Who are they?"
"Dan Marino, Joe Namath, Joe Montana, Jim Kelly, and John Unitas."

Even more impressive. The tight end named all five. Two of them played before he was even born.

The stud put on a show against the Registrar's JV team. Thirteen catches for 221 yards, 2 TDs. We lost 42-22. But, he ran over people, by people, and through people.

Ohhhh, Caaaanada.

"Coach, your tight end and quarterback sure would look good in our uniform next year. What are their plans? We'd like to get them down here for a visit."

The tight end and the quarterback officially became weapons. Artillery. They became our **"communication directors."**

Don't fuck around with the Canadians.

Weapons that could easily get across the border. If a guy can play football at the next level, American university coaches don't care if the player was born in Scandanavia. Global recruiting. Finding weapons — worldwide.

The *Tipping Point* came in the mail the next week. Great book. A have-to-read-it-again book.

∞

Normally, the Niagara X-Men defense is supposed to be the communication director — the team messenger — the marketing department. But not in year one. Not in **1 A.D. (Absence of Defense)**. More weight room was needed. More lifting. More strength.

Strength tilts the playing field. It closes gaps. It causes Culture Shock. The game is about the strong and the weak. And the choices. Which group to join.

In year one, we settled for watching our opponents yell at their defense for letting the Canadians push them around.

"WHERE'S THE PASS RUSH? WHERE'S THE COVERAGE? THEY'RE RUNNING OVER YOUR ASSES!"

There is nothing better that letting the opposing coaches do your trash-talking. Other people brand you. Marketing slogans don't.

∞

Post-game football rituals are like a blend of political rallies, wedding reception lines, and funerals. Handshaking. Mumbling the same thing over and over. Exchanging disingenuous pleasantries.

"Good game... good luck... good game... good luck... good luck... good game..."

The John Wayne look-alike was a welcome reprieve.

"Coach, man y'all had 'em on the ropes. My son is the Thiel QB. I'm a high school coach from Titusville. Just wanted to say I like your style. You're pretty intense for a Canadian."

Pretty intense for a Canadian!

Note to self: Good lecture material.

Post-game speeches can become monotonous.

"I hope you people understand what you are doing! You are single-handedly changing the way an entire country thinks about us. Pretty intense for a Canadian! They think we're a bunch of laid-back yodelers from some juvenile beer commercial! They think we're from Switzerland! Next time we play here, we'll play the game in an alley! A cage! No fans! No scoreboard! We'll show them intensity!"

Actually, if we did ask for a game in an alley or in a cage, they would likely agree. No one is easier to get along with than American football coaches. They're all gentlemen — humble, cordial, professionals. Not one asshole. No mindless, nauseating nostalgia. No macho bravado. No *"you-should-of-seen-us"* blasts from the past. No *"wait-'til-you-see-us-this-year, we're-gonna-kick-your-ass"* play-ground bullying.

Best of all, no politics. Getting games scheduled in the US is the easiest thing we have ever done in football. It costs about $5.50 (US currency) in long distance charges but absolutely no deadly, excessive cortisol secretions.

In Canada, we have league AGMs, commissioners, boards of governors, conference calls, fines, lawyers, shouting, name-calling, threats of civil action. Even articles of impeachment.

"Two-thirds of the vote is all we need to kick them out of the league!"

One time, a "**pox**." Sent out from the league secretary and directed at one of the coaches at a meeting.

"What's a pox?"
"I think it's the same as 'the malocchio' — the evil eye."
"Does that horn thing you Italians wear around your neck work?"

Scheduling a game with a team in the United States: find phone numbers of universities near the Peace Bridge. Dial phone. Talk to head coach.

"We're from Canada. We want to play football in the USA."

No wise-cracks. No trash-talking. No taunting. Strictly business. Respectful. Five minutes tops. Date, time, place. And some of them say:

"And we'll feed your boys after the game."

Just like my Italian relatives. Invite you over. Fight. And then eat.

"We'll wear blue, you wear white. How's that sound? Need directions?"

Game on. Not *"bring it on."* Game on.

"See y'all in September."

And when September comes and they pummel you, they congratulate you.

"Man, you guys have some decent players. We want to talk to #6 and #81. They are weapons. We want to get them here. How do you recruit these boys?"

Recruiting, at the majority of post-secondary schools, is the single-most important element of building a football program. The style — aggressive. Top recruits are the bread and butter of the program. The key to success. Recruit the biggest, fastest, strongest, smartest athletes, and winning is simple.

University recruiting includes endless communication with star high school athletes often culminating in undignified begging for the player to attend the university. The consequence of all this is the intolerable Generation X attitude, the selfish me-first entitlement attitude. Players believe they are above the team. That they are guaranteed everything from a starting job to the position of their choice, and they won't have to work hard for anything. They are the centre of the universe and the world revolves around them.

The Niagara X-Men recruiting strategy is the opposite. Unconventional. Life is too short to beg star athletes to play. We want players who want to be here and who want to make something out of themselves. Players who have drive, balls, and work ethic. Players who are decent, normal, humble student-athletes. They want to be part of a team. Players who love getting into a weight room day after day, month after month, busting their asses even when no one is looking.

Our recruiting strategy is simple. We communicate four things:

1. The existence of the team.
2. The benefits.
3. Past performance — the countless past players who got recruited and advanced to the next level.
4. An invitation to tryout, regardless of size or current skill level.

Instead of pleading with players, a simple message is communicated:

"The only Canadian team that plays exclusively in the US. You can play at an awesome level of football. The opportunity will be life-altering. Transformational."

That's the message. We stay on that message.

"The opportunity to develop will be limitless. Dramatic improvement. Doors will open. But, no guaranteed starting jobs. No guarantee that you will be offered scholarships. No guarantees, with one exception — opportunity. Opportunity is guaranteed. The opportunity to get bigger, stronger, more skilled, and to get recruited. You have to experience it to believe it."

Players then have to make a decision. Take the opportunity or reject it. Maximize it or minimize it. Life is about choices. Life is the by-product of decisions. So is a football career. The Niagara X-Men provide the big stage. Players have to do the rest — work out and practice. Lift weights religiously, run, eat right, and practice. The organization helps a player form positive habits, but it will not force the learning of them. The team will help stretch a player as far as he wants to grow, but will not force him to stay. No coercing, no promises.

We don't cut players. They cut themselves.

We are not an exclusive club that limits membership only to the football upper-class — the superstar high school players. The X-Men are an equal-opportunity team. Everyone has an equal opportunity to sweat their asses off to make their lives better. The good, the bad, and the ugly are all welcome.

The Niagara X-Men believe in the nature versus nurture theory. The vast majority of our former players, who got recruited and moved on, were considered football lower-class athletes. Players are made, not born.

Yes, some athletes are genetically blessed with certain physical gifts that form a foundation for talent. But, as research has proven, talented players are developed. Countless hours of instruction and repetition are needed to develop talent.

This contrarian recruiting strategy is obviously not for every team. Post-secondary football in the United States is big business. Incredible sums of money are at stake. Winning translates into making more money. American football coaches can get fired. This means that they have to recruit only the best.

The X-Men are different. A non-profit "**club**" team. Not one cent of their operating budget comes from public money. The X-Men fundraise to stay alive. That's why our recruiting ideology is different. It's simple and efficient — if you decide to play, you will compete at the best level of football possible. Every game will be filmed. The film will be sent to a large network of university recruiters.

This recruiting strategy creates the great coaching paradox. Noble but draining. No bull but painful. Recruiting only the best athletes — the high-class athlete — would be the faster, easier road. No winding curves. No cliffs. Just a straight, fast track with a high performance machine.

Low maintenance, easy to drive. Start the engine, press the gas pedal, and go. Winning would be much easier. Nice ride but not very rewarding. A fix for the adrenaline junkie but a short-term one.

Transforming a jalopy into a respectable machine takes everything you've got. Everything. You need a lot of tools, a lot of fixing, and when it's ready to drive, you have to grip the steering wheel. Both hands on the wheel. Can't take your eyes off the road for even a split-second. Maneuver through some steep inclines and nasty curves. Some frustrations, even some yelling, but if you don't crash, what a ride!

And, if the transformed jalopy can keep pace with the Indy car…

Vatican@hotmail.com.

∞

No profession creates more memories than one that allows you to transform "**lost causes**" into "**found causes**." Ask St. Jude. No profession builds more good and bad memories than coaching football. For the players and the coaches.

We don't remember what didn't matter. We don't remember what didn't make an impact on them. We don't remember what didn't transform them. But we remember what shocks us. What flicked the switch. What opened the adrenaline floodgates. The *"Holy shit! Did you see that?"* moments and the *"Holy shit! What was I thinking?"* moments.

24-24… 38-36…

"Three eighty-eight!"
"That's a bold statement. No profession is more rewarding and more draining. How can you say that?"

Simple. What's the toughest job on earth? Parenting.

There is nothing harder than shaping a young life because:
1. what's at stake, and
2. there's no training manual.

What's at stake is the development of a life. A human being. There is no blueprint that will help you raise a human being from childhood to adulthood.

Football coaching and parenting are exactly the same with two exceptions — volume and high-risk. A football team is like a huge family of young boys. Imagine forty or fifty 19-year-old boys at your breakfast table. Add the absurd amount of violence associated to the sport. Try to teach them manners while trying to make them monsters.

∞

If you play against monsters long enough, eventually you will play like one.

There is a place in the brain that is rarely visited. It's the room where an athlete, or anyone, can move to when the pain gets too deep. The room is not an escape. Just the opposite. It's a transformer room. A place where next-level preparation happens. To enter, a switch has to be pressed. The switch is not a lock. There is no combination or key that opens it. The switch has to be pressed with sufficient pressure. Once inside, heavy work is done. Heavy lifting, heavy moving. The visit must be temporary. A timely exit is essential. It's vital. Visitors cannot move in permanently and cannot overstay their welcome. In and out.

The visitor leaves with more valuables but less weight. And the switch shuts off until the next time.

∞

The ultimate in football monster play is the "final drive." The up-against-the-wall moment of truth. Gripping drama. Where you move your ass to the edge of the seat. The final act. The last chapter. You get to write it. The chance to find out what you've got.

More specifically, what your offense has got.

Buffalo State ball… third down and six on their 44-yard line… two minutes and 9 seconds left in the game… X-Men losing 38-30.

This qualifies as a "**must stop**" situation in football coaching language. The Niagara X-Men defense must prevent the Buffalo State offence from gaining six yards. They have to get possession of the ball by turnover or by not allowing the ball to be moved six yards. The same X-Men defense that was a non-factor in the past 4 USA games. The same X-Men defense that lacked the muscle to stop any of the previous

4 Goliaths. Got thrown out of the alley. Four times. Physically muscled out. This same X-Men defense has to set the stage so the X-Men offense can have that dramatic "**final drive**."

Failure to stop the Buffalo State offense — allow them to get a first down — will kill the dream of an X-Men final drive. No second chance. No choice. A first down by Buffalo State mathematically would end the game. Buffalo would be able to take a knee and run out the clock. Failure was not an option.

Third and 6 needs a decision. Run or pass against the weak X-Men defense. The decision was not too hard. Actually, it was anti-climatic. Any decision would do. A defense without muscle can't stop anything.

"Settle down, class. Something every good coach should know. Third and 6 means 3rd and long. Understand? It means 3rd and LONG! That means you must pass. When it's 3rd and short, run. Third and LONG, PASS. Now repeat after me. Third and..."

A weak defense has only one hope when it's 3rd and 6 with the game on the line. Pray they put the ball in the air. Hope they pass. Why? Four reasons:

1. A weak defense cannot stop any running play. Period.
2. If they successfully run but don't get the full 6 yards, they still have another chance. A chance called "*4th down.*"
3. A running play would keep the clock ticking. Time was already short.
4. If they put the ball in the air, neither team has possession of the ball. It's the football version of putting it up for grabs. Especially if the team is not a passing team — not one that passes a lot.

The Buffalo State decision should have been a no-brainer. Run. Call a running play. The weakest defense in North American post-secondary football was on the field. Run the ball on 3rd and six.

"Don't worry, coach, maybe they'll lose their minds and call a pass play."
"Are you crazy? They'll call a running play and run straight through us like a hot knife through butter!"

Nope. They blinked. Their short sideline pass fell to the ground. Incomplete. Now, 4th and 6, near midfield. Only 2:02 left.

Go for it for crying out loud! You are Goliath! The guy in front of you is weaker than David! He doesn't even have a slingshot! They are Canadians! First-time tourists! Don't bring a kicker into this battle! Don't bring a David in to fight another David! GO FOR IT!!!

Blink. Again.

They punted.

∞

"If the punt lands inside our 20, DON'T TOUCH IT! GET OUT OF THE WAY! LET IT ROLL!"
"Don't try to catch the punt inside our 20!"
"Why coach?"

WHAT IF YOU FAIL?

PEOPLE WILL TALK IF YOU TRY AND FAIL!

LAUGHERS WILL LAUGH IF YOU TRY AND FAIL!

CRITICS WILL CRITICIZE IF YOU TRY AND FAIL.

SO, DON'T EVEN TRY! GET THE HELL OUT OF THE WAY! BE A TOURIST!! WALK AND GAWK!

"In case you drop it!"

Instead of trying to catch the punt and return it towards the other team's end zone, which is the point of the blessed game,

"LET THE BALL DROP TO THE GROUND!"

Thanks for listening. They can't remember the time the bus leaves but they remember a stupid Coaching 101 rule that teaches fear, anxiety, and stress.

The ball rolled to a stop, deep in our end. Too deep. The striped guy with the line-of-scrimmage stick ran down the opposite sideline. He planted the stick on our 9-yard line. 100 minus 9 equals 91. That's how you figure out distances when you are standing on the opposite sideline.

1 minute 56 seconds left in the game. Down by 8. 91 yards to the end zone. 29 players versus 83. Football is a math exercise.

116 seconds left in a game that no one but next-of-kin was watching. A 91-yard drive with less than two minutes to go — one of the worst final-drive scenarios an offense can face. Double it when the offense is not Goliath.

"Same as we do every practice coach?"

"Yup. Same thing we practice every day. Hammer them! Pound the shit out of them! Go to the body! Do not let them breath! Open the throttle! You know what you're doing."

A polite but redundant quarterback-coach meeting. Short, sweet, to the point. No bullshit.

Translation #1: Here's the car keys.

The quarterback calls all the plays. Spreads the offense. Warp-speed no-huddle. Lightening with thunder. Mid-range to deep passes. There is no such thing as too many too deep passes. No chicken-shit short passes. No running plays. The quarterback is the only runner. The quarterback is a weapon — a cross between a missile and a tank. He should be playing in the US because he works out in the weight room. So should the other weapon — the tight end.

Load… re-load.

Translation #2: See who blinks first.

Throw big punches. No shoving. No pushing. No biting. No purse swinging. Throw bombs. Body shots. Head shots. No hay-makers. Aim each punch. Stay on track, moving forward. Do not move off the track. Someone has to move. And if they happen to punch back, throw bigger bombs.

Load… re-load.

Either way, do not park the missile-launcher.

American football teams are not allowed to lose to Canadians. This would be unthinkable. It's not part of the culture. So, blinking was not an option — for either team.

∞

The final drive was perfect.

91 yards, 1 minute and 56 seconds. Touchdown.

91 yards, 116 seconds. 12 plays. 9 pass plays. 3 runs by weapon #1 — the quarterback. 4 catches by the tight end — weapon #2. Surface-to-surface missiles.

All 12 plays called by the quarterback.

Perfect balance. 58 seconds of actual playing time and 58 seconds in between plays. Mid-range to deep passes. Lightning, warp-speed, no-huddle.

Mathematically and strategically perfect. Just like we had practiced it over and over, for hours, every day, for weeks and months. Players whose uniforms did not fit. Players who were, *"nice kids... not one asshole on the team."* Players who had shown no monster in them — until today.

∞

The final drive confirmed why we do the things we do. Why football is appealing. Why passing within an unconventional spread, warp-speed no-huddle is appealing: rapid-fire, structured improvisation makes you come alive physically, intellectually, and emotionally. The shot of adrenaline that brings you back from the dead.

It took the entire season, but the defense monster'd up. So did the offense. But, one more monster play was needed to finish the deed. To tie the game. Three yards, 2 points, 4 zeros on the clock.

A monster is nothing more than an enigma. We fear enigmas. We fear what we don't know. We fear what we don't understand. Monsters are sons-of-whores who lurk everywhere. Everywhere! Can't escape them.

Monsters have strategy meetings. They pull out their playbooks.

Throw big punches. No shoving. No pushing. No biting. No purse swinging. Throw bombs. Body shots. Head shots. No hay-makers. Aim each punch. Stay on track, moving forward. Do not move off the track. See who blinks first. Someone has to move. And if they happen to punch back, throw bigger bombs.

Either way, do not park the missile-launcher.

Load… re-load.

Bastards.

"388!"

∞

IX
Five Smooth Stones

*"He took his shepherd's stick and then picked up five smooth stones
from the stream and put them in the bag. With the
sling ready, he went out to meet Goliath."*
- 1 Samuel 16:23

*"There was a guy named Greg. He didn't like cops but he never
called us names. Every time we found him in the alley, he would fight.
Never said a word. Just fight. The only people you fear are the ones
that just do it and don't talk about it. And the only people you bring
down the alley are the ones who have done it. Not the ones who just talk
about it. This is like going down the alley."*

Watch what you say to impressionable young athletes. Watch what
you say! Especially the tone. What you say may be remembered. What
you say with passion is remembered.

Greg was the craziest person I ever met during my police career.
A violent recidivist. Robberies, break-ins, drugs, weapons. He busted
his own dad's head during a domestic, then pulled a knife on us when we
got there. But no name-calling. No trash-talking. No wild chest-thumping
"*I'm-gonna-kick-your-ass*" shrieking. Just staring in silence until someone
blinked. No hard feelings afterwards. Greg became a valuable informant.
But the fighting never stopped. Friend, then foe. MDM. Most Dangerous
Man. A scouting report title given to the opposing player who must be
stopped. The guy who can do the most damage. The guy who has to be
defended first and foremost in order to win. Greg's dead now. But his
legacy lives on. Through speeches.

The "**Greg speech**" was the halftime speech in Buffalo, New York.
Fittingly, sirens blared in the background. 24-24. Tie game. The second
half would be a series of alleys leading to the final drive. The ultimate
alley. A "**Greg**" alley.

A dark alley.

∞

"This is the alley!"

Minor miracle, but a miracle nonetheless. The player least likely to enter or even recognize an alley, laid down the gauntlet to the offense right after he did his job on defense.

"We just did our job. Now you do yours. We got the ball back. Do something with it!"

Watch what you say to players… watch what you say. Boomerang communication. Like parrots wearing helmets.

He was part of the 11 players who had made Goliath blink. A believer. Lifetime buy-in. The player least likely to enter an alley suddenly craved another. After just one appearance in that dark alley.

"Hello?"
"Hello. I'm Wally's mother. He has a question. Wally wants to know…"
"Excuse me. How old is Wally?"
"Nineteen."
"Why didn't Wally call?"

Compose email…

To: Parents
Subject: Coddling
Message:
   Stop coddling your grown adult kids.
   Let them walk into alleys — alone.
   Thank you.

He was hooked. A lower-class athlete lifted to the middle-class. One dark alley entered. One dark alley exited. Alive. A dark alley junkie was born. But, now he had to become a spectator on the sidelines and watch the "**final drive.**" The offense's alley. The most unlikely of alleys possibly in the history of dark alleys — in Buffalo, New York.

The only way any final drive can happen is if the gap narrows. The competitive gap. The gap that four weeks earlier had been the size of the Grand Canyon.

The final drive is the football equivalent of the 15th round of a title fight. The 15th round is not guaranteed. It happens only if one guy doesn't get knocked out earlier in the bout. Only if neither player falls into darkness. Just one moment of darkness and the referee starts counting. Waves the arms. Fight's over. No 15th round. No lady in the bikini holding the sign with number 15 on it. Darkness prevention lets the fighter answer the final bell. Getting to the 15th round means keeping the lights on. If the lights are turned off, fight's over. All that preparation for nothing. All that training wasted. Why? Because the 15th round brings you back to life and keeps you alive.

Before every final drive, the quarterback always stops — to talk with the coach — before entering the alley. Muscle memory. Just like on TV. The power of conformity. A coach can predict the outcome of a final drive, during this traditional meeting, by simply making direct eye contact with the quarterback. Look for fight or flight. It's easy to recognize which one is happening. Watch for blinking.

None seen. He never blinked. No panic. No flight. Just fight. This from the same kid who couldn't even make direct eye contact five weeks ago.

"You know, you can't change a leopard's spots."

Yes you can.

∞

"Clock Management" is part of the postmodern football vernacular. It is a component of the offense's final drive strategy. A relationship between time and distance. Rules expertise is a necessity to manage the clock. Know when to stop it, know when to start it. The key is to conserve time by doing something that stops the clock as long as possible until the next play or at least until the referee places the ball. There are three primary ways to **"stop the clock"** until the next snap: timeout, incomplete pass, and running out of bounds.

Each team gets three timeouts per half. A good clock manager has learned how to call a timeout.

"Press the fingertips of one hand into the palm of the other hand to form a 'tee' while yelling, 'TIMEOUT! TIMEOUT!' You can't simply press the fingertips into the palm. You must wildly bounce the palm on and off the fingertips while shrieking 'TIMEOUT!' Repeat the bouncing and the shrieking until the ref acknowledges you."

Passing failure also stops the clock. An incomplete pass stops the clock until the next play. A positive from a negative.

Running out of bounds is usually frowned upon except in relation to clock management. It stops the clocks but it also limits the amount of distance gained and it questions the courage of the runner.

"He ran out of bounds. He must have no balls."

The football field is the only place where avoiding a collision brings on whispers of the "C" word.

"Officer, the other driver was in my lane so I smashed head-on into the car instead of swerving!"
"Attaboy. That showed some real balls."

"Football balls" is measured by the volume and nature of the collision.

"Officer, I drove into the ditch to avoid a head-on collision with a car that was in my lane."
"Chickenshit."

But on the final drive, this negative becomes a positive. Running out of bounds stops the clock all the way until the next play. Avoiding collisions is preferred during the final drive.

"Get the hell out of bounds! What do you think you're doing colliding with that linebacker!?"

Must be confusing for players. When to crash. When to swerve. Wreckage. No wreckage.

Gaining a first down stops the clock — temporarily. Not all the way until the next play though. It stops the clock only until the guys holding the 10-yard chains on the sideline jog (plod?) to re-position the chain. When the chain crew is done and the 10-yard sticks are planted in the ground, the referee places the ball and blows the whistle to start the clock again — before the quarterback starts the cadence and well before the ball is snapped. A positive from a positive. Every second counts.

There is a myth in football fantasyland that you can **"manage the clock"** on game day with prior planning. With a script. You can't. No script works for one simple reason — no one can predict the outcome

4TH & HELL SEASON 1

of any single play. Not the first play, the second, or the last. To manage the clock going forward, you need to know the outcome of the previous play. There is a relationship between what just happened and what comes next. The immediate future depends on the immediate past. General pre-planning is fine, but improvisation is more important. Structured improvisation. Rapid-fire decision-making. A revised strategy is needed after each play because the time/distance relationship changes after each play. No two situations during a final drive will ever be the same. Warp-speed strategic improvisation. Lightning-fast decision-making is the key to survival. More natural selection.

The **"two-minute drill"** is another football game myth. The infamous drill that can allegedly transform a plodding run-oriented team that huddles after every play, into a warp-speed no-huddle passing monster. Like trying to make a jet out of a tractor.

What you focus on grows. What you do most becomes who you are. What you rarely do regresses. You can't reach a level of performance without practicing it deliberately and often. You can't suddenly become a fierce air force for 2 minutes when you **"ground and pound"** for the previous 58.

We don't have a two-minute drill. Twenty years ago, we decided to make the whole game a two-minute drill. Hang on, grip hard, white knuckle stuff. Our offense was designed as a series of two-minute drills. And we gave it a name — **SWAT. Speed With Attitude Team. Strength With Attitude Team.** A spread, no-huddle full-game two-minute drill. It's a 60-minute workout with no rest between sets. A natural selection process. The no-huddle approach defines strength and speed.

Everyone is strong and fast on the first play. That's expected. Everyone is at their peak right after the national anthem. They're comfortable, dressed in their Sunday best. Clean clothes. Hair combed. But, it really doesn't matter who is stronger or faster at the beginning of a game — during the 1st round. What matters is who remains fastest and strongest — physically and mentally — as the game progress. All the way to the 15th round.

After working hard. What matters is who manages fatigue better. Who can handle less recovery time. Who can play hard when the rest/recovery time is next to nothing. Who can deal with discomfort better. Discomfort forces a decision. Keep swinging or throw in the towel. Answer the bell or stay on the stool. Get up or get counted out.

Strength-deficit management. Who can deal with fatigue better. Who can take deeper gulps of air when the lungs are burning. When the lights are going out. When the shades are slowly lowering. Just before the total eclipse.

A no-huddle offense is the equivalent of relentless body shots. Who will survive the 15th round? Who will even get there? A no-huddle sends a message:

"Don't let them breathe. Don't let them think. Keep pounding fast and furiously. To the body, to the head. See how much they can take."

Bring it to them, instead of having it brought to you.

∞

The no-huddle paradox.

A warp-speed no-huddle is a great way to avoid darkness.

Full-throttle.

Load… re-load.

It keeps the lights on. Like an ancient generator. Keep moving and the lights stay on full blast. Slow down and it gets dim — until it gets so dark that you can't move around without smashing into things, knocking things down. Crashing and bashing. Wreckage and carnage.

But the lightning sparked by a no-huddle offense can almost be blinding. Momentarily. Or longer. And no-huddle lightning always comes first, before the thunder. Deep, rolling thunder. The kind that scares the shit out of you. Makes you jump. But, never vice versa. The thunder never comes before the lightning when you try to light it up with a relentless no-huddle. Lightning first, thunder second.

Lightning has poor aim. No programmed GPS coordinates. No specific target. It hits whatever is in the wrong place at the wrong time. If you make lightning, run like hell out of the way. Because, if it strikes you…

"Get to the line! SPRINT TO THE LINE! LINE-UP!"

The language of a no-huddle coach.

"GET UP! RUUUUNNNN TO THE LINE! LINE-UP!"

The language of a no-huddle coach.

"Can we slow it down when we're winning? You know... huddle? Can we huddle when we're ahead? To take a break?"

"Absolutely not! We never slow down. NEVER!"

The language of a no-huddle coach.

"I don't care if we're up by 36 points! Doesn't matter! Get back to the line as fast as you can! Don't waste one blessed second!"

We tried to huddle once. In the fourth quarter of a game in Canada played before our decision to play exclusively across the border.

"Ok, we're winning by 28 points. We need to kill the clock. Scrap the no-huddle. Slow it down. Huddle after each play. Use up as much time as possible."

It was an embarrassment. Disjointed huddle. Players bumping into each other. Withdrawal symptoms. Darkness. Boredom. Too much time on their hands between plays. Drove them nuts.

No one knew what to do. Like methamphetamine addicts trying to go cold turkey. Twitching. Tugging hair. Fetal position. Like filling kids with sugar before Sunday Mass then getting pissed off when they don't sit still in the Church pew. Eye-gouging mom and dad, running onto the altar...

"GO BACK TO NO-HUDDLE!"

Instant calm.

∞

The final drive often brings out the **"prevent defense."** Another myth. A strategy that is almost never used for 58 minutes in a game. It is a soft, passive defensive strategy. Defenders line up deeper than normal, sprint backwards at break-neck speeds, trying to prevent the defense's worst nightmare — the dreaded deep pass completion.

Defensive coaches shriek countless fear-provoking paranoia-generating warnings.

"Don't let any receiver get past you! Stay deep for cryin' out loud!"
"NO DEEP PASSES!"
"DO... NOT... LET... THEM... SCORE!"

The equivalent of Goliath's coaches shrieking:

"BACK UP, dagnabit! That scrawny David's got a slingshot and 5 smooth stones! DO... NOT... LET... HIM... KNOCK... YOU... OUT! BAAAACCCCKKKKK UP!"

The equivalent of a 15th round dance. Where one fighter moves away — no, runs away — from the other fighter trying not to get punched. Avoiding engagement instead of trying to knock the other guy out.

The equivalent of two guys in an alley and one backing up all the way to the back door of the alley. Backing up, step after step, giving the other guy room to move. Room to attack.

"Back up! Can't you see he's coming at you?"

Things get tough? Back up. 15th round? Back up. Final drive? Back up. Stare eyeball-to-eyeball? Back up. Mobile blinking.

"Don't fight back, don't... fight... back! Back up!

The "prevent defense" tries to prevent a negative instead of causing a positive. It doesn't work. The prevent defense does not stop a spread no-huddle high-power passing offense. It only prevents only thing — defense. It prevents defense from happening. The prevent defense becomes a facilitator. It allows a spread offense to pass at will.

If all these defensive strategies don't work. What does? A two-step proactive strategy.

Step #1. Flatten the QB while he his holding the ball. Before he passes. In football language, this is called a *"sack."*

A sack has three benefits. First, it's gotta hurt. Guys with big muscles sprinting full speed into a quarterback who is standing still, knocking the quarterback on his ass. The QB will likely think twice before holding onto the ball that long the next time.

134

Secondly, the offense loses yards instead of gaining yards. Positions the offense farther away from the end zone that they are trying to enter.

Third, the clock keeps ticking. The clock does not stop on a quarterback sack. This adds insult to injury, really throwing off the **"Clock Management Script."**

"Look, our quarterback just got slammed to the ground. He's on his ass. Flat on his ass! Can you at least stop the clock to let him dust himself off?"

"No, the clock keeps moving. You're losing time. Time will not stop just because you got knocked on your ass. If you want to save time, get off your ass as fast as possible. The longer you stay on the ground, the more time you lose. The more time you waste. It takes a few seconds to get off your ass. And there are 10 teammates to reach out with a hand to pull you up. So, you have a choice. Get off your ass or lay on your ass. Either way, the clock's moving."

The next best thing to a sack is a "**hurry**." This is football language for a near-sack. The quarterback did throw the pass but he threw it before he wanted to. He was in a rush caused by a pass rush. A negative rush caused by a positive rush.

Step #2. Flatten the receivers as they leave the line of scrimmage. Some football coaches call this "bump & run." Smashing the receivers at the line prevents (no pun intended) receivers from running around at full speed wherever they want to go. It's uncomfortable for the receivers.

This tactic has three benefits. First, it's gotta hurt. Second, it frustrates the receivers. Frustration tends to screw up thinking, resulting in doing stupid things. Third, it disrupts the offense's plans. It disrupts the timing of the pass play. The receiver gets knocked off his path so he won't get to where he's supposed to be at the specified time. This causes the quarterback to search wildly and panic when he can't find the receiver. Stress. Anxiety. Disorder. Leads to a sack. And if the sack is hard enough, it may lead to darkness.

PRESSURE! Constant pressure. Sacks, hurries, bump & run… all forms of intense pressure.

Hurries and sacks send a bad news/good news message:

"This is not going to be easy. You will not be given room to move. You won't be given enough time. Things will get dim. It may even get dark. It won't stop. They're going to keep coming. There will be every attempt to knock you to the ground. On to your ass. Think of it as a test — to see if you can handle the pressure. If you can stay standing. And if you do get knocked down, can you get up? And if you do get up, the whole thing starts all over. More pressure. More knockdown attempts."

Good news: If you learn to handle the pressure, you will move the ball. You'll move it far. There will be less traffic downfield where the ball is caught. Less traffic means more room to move towards the goal-line.

Prescription for Pressure? Protection. Blockers. Those guys upfront called "**the offensive line.**" The inner circle. Those who will build not just a brick wall but a mountain around their quarterback. Those who will unselfishly use every vicious hand-to-hand combat tactic known to mankind to protect their passer. To give the quarterback enough time to throw the ball so that the receiver can catch it and make something happen. To make sure each play reaches its potential.

And they do this without any real recognition. Blockers don't get their names in the paper. Quarterbacks and receivers do. Blockers go back to the weight room to lift and get even stronger, because the next opponent will try even harder. The next opponent will invent a new strain of Pressure. Blockers do all the heavy lifting in anonymity. Naturally. No unnatural help. There is no other solution. No magic formula in a bottle that can protect the QB better than a strong offensive line.

A weak offensive line will wilt under pressure. The quarterback will get sacked. Maybe killed. Lazy, complacent blockers are not blockers. They are co-conspirators. They are part of an organized effort to destroy the quarterback. Uninspired, uncommitted blockers are tourists — "**watchout**" tourists. They yell, "*watch out*" to the quarterback just as he's ready to get whacked.

There is a cure for a weak offensive line — lifting — heavy lifting. One day at a time. One set at a time. One rep at a time. Natural selection.

Does football imitate life? Or does life imitate football?

Is football stranger than life? Or is life stranger than football?

∞

Prevent defense is a slang term for zone coverage — soft zone coverage. Essentially, the defensive coach decides to not cover receivers man-to-man. Instead, he sends seven defenders sprinting, backwards, each to a spot on a field. From there, they react to where the ball is thrown. Soft zone creates room — giant vacant open areas — on the field. It allows receivers to slightly alter their routes so they can sprint in a giant, open room and it affords the quarterback an easy time finding open receivers in those giant, open areas.

Soft zone usually means that only four defenders are rushing the quarterback. Against five blockers. Four rushers versus five blockers equals minimal or no pressure. The quarterback will not get flattened. Should not get flattened. A good security plan.

Soft zone coverage is a quarterback's dream. No rush, open area. Freedom. Put the ball in the air. Or, keep it and run with it. Freedom. Less pressure. More productivity… today. But less long-term growth. Prevent defense actually harms the offense in the long run. Hinders offensive development. No pressure — no growth.

The best learning experience comes from pressure. Not from softness. Pressure creates balls, enlarges them, makes them hard. Heavy metal. BOSS — **B**alls **O**f **S**tainless **S**teel. Soft coverage will make the offense look good today but eventually, no improvement. Leading to regression.

∞

The problem with dreams is there are two kinds. The first type is the kind that makes absolutely no sense. The kind that we wake up from after they scare the shit out of us. This type of dream drives us to www.dreaminterpretation.ca.

Search…
White horse galloping, through my office, my dead uncle as the rider, I'm free-falling from…

These dreams are dark or cloudy.

"All I remember is a zebra with a smug look laughing but I can't remember what it was saying or anything else."

These dreams may be embarrassing.

"I was yelling 388 on a field and people were shocked and..."

These dreams are not always inspiring.

"I walked into this room. Full of bars and weights. It was lonely. No one showed up."

The line between that type of dream and a nightmare gets blurred.

The second type of dream is not cloudy or hazy and doesn't happen during sleep. It is clear. Lightning clear. It happens while we're wide awake. This type of dream does make sense. Complete sense. It is our inner sense. This type of dream is supposed to be inspiring but we are fully capable of turning it into a full-fledged horror movie where we are producer, director, and star. A murder mystery. Where the killer is known right from the beginning and the reason for the homicide is the only mystery. The only suspense is whether the dead comes alive. Will the dead dream resurrect?

One type of dream happens during sleep. The other is put to sleep.

∞

There is a street fight between "**extreme**" and "**balance**."

"Get out your Coaching 201 textbook. Page 3. See, you gotta have a balanced offense! 50-50. Gotta run and pass the same amount. 50-50!"

We define "**balance**" differently. Balance is doing what works. Getting the job done. Even if it goes to extreme. Extreme becomes balance when it works. When it doesn't, it's an out-of-control high-performance machine.

This final drive was perfect. X-game style. Extreme. To the Xth degree.

Twelve total plays. Ninety-one yards. Touchdown.

Nine of the plays were pass plays using five receivers — the maximum amount legally allowed. Extreme. Extreme spread offensive strategy. No actual running plays called. Three running plays happened when the quarterback ran with the ball after he couldn't find open receivers. X-game running plays — pass plays that don't work. More extremes. 75%-25% pass-run ratio but 100% pass play-calling. Off-the-charts extreme.

And it worked — this time. It achieved an unprecedented time balance. The 116 seconds remaining in the game divided equally — 58 seconds of actual playing time and 58 seconds of non-playing time (the wasted time between plays – the time that has to be conserved). Perfect "**Clock Management**." The touchdown was scored with no time left on the clock — this time.

The X-game worked. Extremes turned into balance. Everything stayed under control. No micro-managing. Slingshot worked. Four zeros showed as the runner entered the end zone. 38-36. Down by only two. No wild celebration. There was still business to take care of. One more play. The two-point conversion.

Goliath had stayed in the soft zone. The prevent defense.

"Back up..... BACK UP!"

Dream rubbing its eyes, lifting its ass out of bed.

David used 5 receivers.

Goliath caught it right in the forehead.

Pow! Culture Shock! Both ways. Two-way simultaneous Culture Shock. Both sides never expected this. Both teams had officially crossed into foreign territory.

∞

How long to make a miracle? According to the laws of miracles, there are no mandatory minimums. There is no compulsory time limit or duration for an event to be classified as a miracle. No rule that says a miracle must last for more than 2 minutes, more than 2 hours.

There is no compulsory distance that must be traveled for a miracle to happen either. No rule that says X number of miles, errr… kilometers.

116 seconds is enough.

"How many miracles is this guy applying for anyway?"

So is 91 yards. Doesn't seem far, but 91 yards is, well, miraculous.

"What is the rule? One application per miracle? Or can you join multiple miracles on one application?"

116 seconds. It takes more time than that to stand in line to order doughnuts. 116 seconds of transformational lightning. And thunder. And shock.

But a 116-second miracle can be easily forgotten; even cancelled. It depends on what happens next. It's the next play that matters. The last play. The last play either makes the previous plays memorable or "**delete**" is pressed. What happens next gives meaning to what happened before.

And what happens last is remembered. Or, what is the most shocking is remembered. Miracles are evaluated by shock value.

∞

Keeping score is a man-made way to quantify success. An artificial way of defining winners and losers. Accumulate the most points and you're a winner. Near-points don't count. No. You must cross the line to score points. Falling short of the line doesn't count in score-keeping. Even if you had to fight like a sonuvabitch to get near the line. Close doesn't count. That's why keeping score is man-made.

With one play left, keeping score tells you the distance needed to climb. 38-36 means three yards to get two points.

But really, 38-36 means 51% - 49%. Enough to get in the White House... or Parliament. Enough to graduate. Enough to be officially classified as a winner — artificially.

∞

There is no manual that tells you what to do when Culture Shock sets in. Culture Shock does not produce one single symptom. No neat sequence of predictable outcomes.

Goliath scratched his head on the opposing sideline. David readied his slingshot.

Load... re-load.

X-game.

"Here's an idea. Call the same thing that just worked — 5 receivers. Spread offense. And, pass. It worked perfectly for the past 116 seconds. My guess is that it should work again, right now, just a measly few seconds later."

Smart-ass rational voice!

If Culture Shock is capable of shutting down rational thought, then they should shut down the border in the name of Homeland Security.

"388!"

∞

X
X = Infinity

"Everybody acts not only under external compulsion but also in accordance with inner necessity."
- Albert Einstein

There is no concrete definition for "**happy ending**." The possibilities are infinite. Some happy endings include, but are not limited to, anything:

1. Electrifying — that plugs us in and charges us up.
2. Asslifting — that moves us, moves us up. Asslifting is uplifting.
3. That doesn't piss us off or bring darkness like… any news broadcast, anywhere, anytime.

"Tonight… breaking news… The end of the world is about to happen. We have live reports from every corner of the earth showing nothing but gloom and doom. But first, the weather. It's getting cloudy. Very cloudy. Not quite total darkness but pretty close. Now back to Armageddon."

One thing is for sure — a happy ending has to be the start of something. It's not really a finish line; it's a starting point.

∞

Who says that a happy ending has to happen after the very last play? Why not before the last play? Either immediately before the last play or even way before it? What about a happy ending before the conventional ending followed by the next play that seems to be the last play but the conventional last play is really the beginning of the sequel, i.e., Part 2?

"Welcome to Writing 101. First rule. Happy endings must happen on the last page. Not before. Never. It must be the very last thing. Ok, repeat after me until it is deeply ingrained. Happy endings must…"

Why do happy endings have to be at the very end of a story? Why can't they happen during a story? Who says that happy endings are reserved for when there's "four zeros on the clock?" Why do we need rigid rules about happy endings?

"Class, let's read from the football story-telling scrolls: Happy endings shall only be at the end!"

"Can there be more than one happy ending? One before the last play and one after the last play?"

"No. Absolutely not. Lemme unravel the scrolls... look here, it says: 'One happy ending per story.'"

"How happy does an ending have to be to qualify as a certified happy ending?"

"Errr... 15 minute break!"

"What if the happy ending hap---"

"WHAT IF YOUR AUNT HAD BALLS, WOULD SHE BE YOUR UNCLE!?"

∞

Driving with your face stuck in the rear-view mirror is deadly. Driving forward, safely, requires keeping your eyes looking ahead. At times, it will be necessary to glance in the rear-view mirror. To see what's behind. To learn from it. Extremely valuable information can be learned from glancing in the rear-view mirror. But all you need is a glance. Not a stare. A glance. Because obsessive zombie-like staring in the rear-view mirror has potentially horrifying consequences.

Fixation with the rear-view mirror causes broken focus. Eyes off the road. Can lead to a crash. A collision. Probably to a very bad wreckage.

The rear-view mirror helps remind us that what is behind is important — it's where we came from. The curves, the hills, the slips and the sliding. And those great road trips that enlightened. But no one can drive forward safely by gawking in the rear-view mirror.

∞

Shocks have a wide range of causes.

There is the brute strength/brute force kind.

"Ooooooh, what a hit! Stretched him right out! I think he's out cold! That'll make the hi-lite reels."

Then there's speed.

"Ran right by him! He looks stunned!"

144

Electric.

"116! 91 yards in 116 seconds!"

Cultural. That bone-crushing impact caused by unfamiliarity. By uncertainty.

"What's your citizenship?"

The outcome of each of the first three types of shock is simple: Physical pain, emotional pain, extreme pleasure. Horror, more horror, and happiness.

But the potential outcomes of the fourth kind of shock are infinite. The outcomes of Culture Shock depend on how the next play unfolds. And the next play. And the next play. The effects of Culture Shock are not immediately known. Sure, some superficial effects are visible. But the deep effects depend on what happens next. The next level. How deep Culture Shock goes depends on what is done with the lessons learned from the Culture Shock. The effects can go deep, too deep, or not deep at all.

One thing is certain about Culture Shock. Uncertainty may cause uncertainty. That's why **"uncertainty management"** is vital. How uncertainty is managed determines how uncertain or certain we are about what we know, what we do, and how we do it.

∞

The strangeness of an unfamiliar place can silence the inner self. It can shut off the inner voice, the communications director of the inner self. It happens in stages. The volume doesn't simply get shut off abruptly. There is no on/off switch that shuts up the inner self with a sneaky push, from far away, of a remote control button. No. The volume gets lowered so slowly, so gradually, that it's perfectly obvious that the voice is softening. No surprise, no suddenness. It's unmistakable. The finger that is lowering the volume belongs to the inner self's owner. No one else can put his hand on the volume button. No one else can silence the inner voice. Only the owner can.

That's why softening is so obvious. The offender is known and the crime is in progress. The offender is not wearing a disguise. No lineup needed. The offender is pointing directly at himself.

"Hey stupid… It's me… IT'S ME!"

The owner knows that the softening can be stopped at any time. By either taking his finger off the volume button or raising the volume level. But instead, the softening is ignored. He looks the other way. Or stalls.

"Pardon?"

The scholarly word to describe "**ignoring the suspect of a crime in progress**" is "**negligence.**" Street language is harsher: "**Chickenshit.**"

"Don't pretend you didn't hear me."

A chickenshit hopes the suspect leaves on his own.

"Maybe the suspect will change his mind."

No. The inner-self volume-softener is relentless.

"Hey, chickenshit. I know you see me. I'm not leaving. You'll have to drag me outta here."

All name-calling starts some kind of a struggle. You hurt me. I hurt you back.

"You're a chickenshit!"
"No, YOU'RE a chickenshit!"

The next stage of conflict mis-management is challenge. Laying down the gauntlet.

"Ya?"
"Ya."
"Oh, ya?"
"Yaaaa!"

No solution, no harmony. If someone doesn't stop the offender from completely shutting off the inner self, the crime escalates because the conflict RPMs rev up. Sand gets thrown. Then, the messenger-bags start swinging. Followed by pushing, shoving, biting. Deeper name-calling.

"You asshole!"

Eventually, punches get thrown. Haymakers. Accompanied by their long-time companion:

"I hate you!"

If someone doesn't intervene, the owner is capable of muffling the inner self, strangling it, mangling it beyond recognition. Disorientation by displacement. Confucktion by convention.

The inner self goes missing.

"When was the last time you heard your real inner self?"

When the inner self doesn't return, the victim tries an APB.

"All cars. Missing inner self. May be armed and dangerous."

The APB is a waste of time — it should have been limited to one person. Everyone already knew what was going on. Everyone had already told the owner where to find it.

"It's right here! What a stench. Looks like this inner self has been decomposing for a long time. Way past the rigor mortis stage. Get the chalk and yellow tape."

This homicide is easy to solve. The suspect is obvious. Someone with a lot of strength. Wasted strength. Incredible strength is needed to overpower the inner self. Inner-self killers have misguided strength. The equivalent of David aiming the slingshot at himself and pelting stones off his own forehead — repeatedly. In public view. With everyone telling him to stop.

Including Goliath.

"Look, David... I'm bored. I need a new challenge. You seem to have huge potential. Why don't you consider directing your attack away from yourself instead of toward yourself? You're wasting your strength."

Uncertainty mis-management may lead to the unnatural death of the inner self and the inner voice. But re-engineered mis-management could lead to new life for both. Stronger, more powerful. Inner self 2.0. With new and improved body armour. How?

"Ok, end-of-the-month uncertainty management reports are due."
"Who do we hand them in to?"
"Yourself. Report to yourself."

∞

Five receivers spread out, lined up wide, is a paradox. It is a way to load and re-load but it also brings on a feeling of emptiness. Loneliness. That's why it's also called an "empty backfield." The quarterback is all alone. No running backs. Minimal protection. No extra blockers. Five receivers. Five blockers. One quarterback. It takes the guesswork away from the defense. The play will likely be a pass play. If not, the quarterback will be the runner.

But, it's a great strategy — potentially. If there's enough protection. If no one sacks the quarterback. If the pressure is managed properly.

Five receivers sprinting horizontally, vertically spaced apart, equally. Like 5 slingshots firing 5 stones simultaneously. It has the potential to be deadly. Explosive capacity, if the explosion happens far enough away from the quarterback. Someone is always open. Always. In fact, at least two receivers are always open. Regardless of defensive coverage. Man-to-man coverage or zone coverage. Doesn't matter. Receivers are always open. Never fails. It's a thing of beauty. The only problem is that the quarterback has to find the open receiver. Not only does he need strong protection from being flattened, he has to have big balls while holding the ball. The quarterback must be able to ignore the pressure. The stress of the hunting party. Those who want to take him apart. Rip him apart and beat him down.

The quarterback has to ignore all the nasty people who want to harm him and focus on his team. Find the open receiver. Find the target. Throw the ball to the open target. Burning focus. Passion. Determination. He cannot blink. Stand straight. Eyes on the targets. Searching for the open man.

Great quarterbacks do not know how to blink. Like they've had their blinking capacity surgically removed. Unfortunately, some quarterbacks have blink implants. Bigger and bigger blinks. They keep growing until there's a risk of an explosion.

Balls prevent blinking.

∞

The popularity of the spread offense has spread. What once was considered high-risk has become part of a postmodern football transformation. The 5-receiver "**spread**" formation is now fashionable. High-octane but doesn't harm the environment.

For decades the conventional formation included only 2 wide-receivers. The other three were lined up in close-quarters. One at "**tight end.**" Two in the backfield as running backs. A nice balance. A safe balance. The problem was that defenses learned how to stop this type of offense because that's what they saw repeatedly. What you focus on grows.

Eventually, someone decided to spread out this close-knit group. Three receivers. Four. How about 5? It worked. Now it's the growing rage in university and high school football. David see. David do.

More slingshots, more stones. More stones, more chances to smack Goliath right between the eyes.

This is why the majority of American universities who have won national championships, in the 21st century, have used the spread offense. That's why the spread offense is now all the rage. That's why the final drive worked.

That's why it was a perfect call for the two-point conversion.

∞

Simplicity recognition: A vital skill. The ability to recognize what is simple.

Ignoring simplicity: A disease. The inability to recognize what is simple. The need to complicate what is simple.

∞

"He's wide open... great pass... it's caught! HE CAUGHT IT! The two-point conversion worked. TIE GAME!"
"Great call coach!

Overtime!

A great fantasy. A wild fantasy to kill time while stopped in line at the Peace Bridge, waiting to re-enter Canada. Some dreams are pleasant. Some are nightmares. Some wake you up with a smile. Some make you scream in horror.

"How long away?"

Canadian border guards are not any friendlier than American border guards. No eye contact. Just, the obligatory scowl. It must be part of the training manual — act pissed off. Never smile.

"Four full quarters plus a damn two-point conversion."
"Bringing anything back?"
"Grief. Regret."
"Go ahead."

There is no duty on grief and regret. No GST. No taxes. *"Go ahead."* You don't even get pulled over for inspection. Should have been pulled over. And questioned. If football were deeply ingrained in Canadian culture like hockey, a full-fledge interrogation would have been appropriate.

"Give us one good reason. Why? Why the hell did you do it? 388? Freeze option?"
"I want my lawyer."
"Look, get it off your chest. You'll feel better."
"I want my phone call."

"388" should be cause for border detention. Or, at least a trip to the emergency room for assessment under the Mental Health Act.

"Who did this to you?"
"It was Culture Shock doctor... You gotta believe me!"
"Sorry. I'm signing a sec. 17 detention order. Seventy-two hour examination."

But no. Instead, you pay $3.25 (Canadian funds) and they let you back into Canada.

At the very least, someone should have asked if it worked. Someone should have asked, *"What really happened?"*

"Passport... and did 388 work? Tell us the truth!"

Confession heals a rotted soul. Honesty out — honesty in.

"This is what really happened. Snap was clean. The quarterback got the ball and faked a hand-off to the fullback so he could decide to run with the ball or pitch it to the tailback. But then, the quarterback slipped and got flattened. At the same time, the unblocked outside linebacker

flattened the tailback. The ball bounced on the ground and came to rest between the flattened quarterback and the flattened tailback. Goliath recovered the ball. Smothered it. Took possession of the loose ball. The whistle blew. The play died. Failed two-point try. Zero points. Then, I got punched in the gut... at least it felt like it. The other team celebrated — wildly. Like they had just won the lottery. Their wild celebration wasn't meant to be insulting. It was the product of intense relief. Of not having to suffer the worst kind of Culture Shock imaginable. The intense relief of not having to explain how the hell Americans lost a football game to a bunch of first year Canadians — the St. Jude club team of football."

That statement should have been required to re-enter Canada. The truth and nothing but the truth. But, the loss of a football game is not mourned in Canada. After all, it's not Texas. No community revolt on the horizon.

"Did you buy any alcohol or tobacco?"
"No, the only deadly item was 388. Didn't buy it. Made it."
"No duty on stupid calls. Especially those made in the USA. Did you leave anything behind?"
"Depends on the next play."
"Welcome back to Canada. Come on in. Have a nice day."

∞

"YOU GOTTA HURT AFTER YOU LOSE!"

Conventional coaching instructions after a loss. Imploring an entire group to act the same, think the same. Trying to spread conformity.

"WIPE THAT SMILE OFF YOUR FACES! YOU LOST!"

More conventional wisdom. Blend into the mainstream. Lose yourself. Be like everyone else. The traditional reprimand to players who do not display sufficient suffering and uncontrolled grief after a football loss.

"As we wind down Coaching 201, let's review a few things: When the score shows you lost, it's a bad ending. An un-happy ending. The worst kind. Make damn sure all your players are unhappy... and show it. It's impossible to be happy after another team scores more points than yours. Remind players to be dark, especially if you see them acting happy."

Losers are supposed to grieve. Compulsory grieving. Losses are supposed to evoke deep intense feelings of hurt. If not, you're not committed and not a real athlete. You must be depressed. Inconsolable.

"GET AWAY FROM ME UNTIL I CALM DOWN! JUST LOST A FOOTBALL GAME!"

Maturity is a big deal in athletics. It is sought after. Pursued relentlessly. That's why amateur sports exist. To make a dent. To get outside ourselves. Do something bigger. All coaches want to see some movement toward players' maturity as a season progresses. Even if it's inch-by-inch. Some sign of growing up. Some beacon of hope. Learning to deal with disappointment. To turn disappointment into an appointment. An appointment with new opportunity.

Some 19-year-olds know how. Some don't. Some face unthinkable tragedy and horror every day in this world. Hunger. Disease. War. Some don't.

"Coach, he took my number."
"What number?"
"My jersey number. I always wear 51. It's my girlfriend's favourite number."
"How old are you?"
"Nineteen."

Some 20-year-olds have reached the age typed on their birth certificate. Some have not.

"Coach, I can't come to the game tomorrow."
"Why not, Jimmy? You took all the reps at that position, all week, all season? Your teammates are counting on you. Are you hurt?"
"No. It's my grandma's birthday. I gotta go or my mom'll be mad."
"How old are you?"
"Twenty."

Pre-season is enough to knock down a healthy rhinoceros.

"I can't run any more coach. (Huff, huff)"
"Why not? That was only the second sprint? You are a healthy young man blessed with every working part."
"I gotta get in shape first."
"But you should have been in shape before you got here."

"I know, but things got busy."
"So, you come to camp out of shape. How old are you?"
"Nineteen."

Listening to sideline chatter during the first game of the season is enough to hospitalize a weaker person.

"Like, did you see the awesome picture I posted on Facebook? Like, man, we got all drunk like, man, at that party, like, someone like took the picture, like, man."
"Like, no way. Like, I haven't like checked it out yet, dude."
"Hey, you two... you're supposed to be on the kickoff team!"

∞

"Good game... good luck... good luck... good game."

The obligatory post-game handshaking. Same stuff. Except for a strong wind — the monster-sized sigh of relief coming from Goliath's direction. And the full-blast ear-splitting wireless message:

"ONLY TWO POINTS. BETCHA YOU CRAPPED YOURSELVES, EH?"

Non-verbal communication is potent.

"Holy cow, coach... your guys GOT HEART! REAL CHARACTER! We got to get some of them here next year!"

Translation: *What a happy ending. I was shocked at the end of that final drive. Now, I'm extremely happy I don't have to explain for 365 days why we Americans lost to 29 Canadians.*

Then silence. No one had to be told to huddle for the post-game speech. No yelling. No micromanaging. No, *"GET IN HERE DAMNIT!"*

No tears. No anguish. No helmet-throwing. No child-like grief.

Instead, they sprinted in on their own — maturely — to the 35-yard line. Huddled and waited.

"Move to mid-field... Stand right on the Bengal."

All 29 moved in unison from the 35-yard line, right on top of the host's painted mascot. A little non-grieving childishness is acceptable.

"Look at the scoreboard! You made them shit themselves! You put them in shock!"

One of their coaches joined our post-game speech.

Smartest lecturer I had ever heard. Twenty years ago. Heard him explain blocking fundamentals. He politely endured phone call after phone call for two decades.

"Ok, what if the tackle lines up over the... What if... ?"

He never once snapped. Never yelled, *"What if the Queen had balls, would she be King?"* He tolerated every *"what if"* question. Answered every one. His advice was the tipping point.

"Does it work for you?"
"Oh ya! It's working!"
"Then keep doing it."

Introducing a legend from the other team during your post-game speech is powerful.

"Our guys shit themselves at halftime. And again at the end of the game. Unbelievable game. Be proud. You're a great team."

No roar. No trash-talk. Just applause. Mature clapping. Just like the team code of conduct says. Respect the game. Respect the opponent.

51% to 49%. The real score. In the infinite wisdom of the academic world, 49% is a failure. Didn't pass. No credit. No re-write. Is 50% the real dividing line? Do two points really matter? Is two points the real difference between success and failure?

∞

Not all Culture Shocks are created equal. But, they can work together. They can join forces. The Law of Unintended Consequences. One Culture Shock sets another one in motion, forming a chain. Links have to be added. Some strong, some weak. Some smart, some stupid.

"388!"

A ripple effect. The ripples keep rippling — wider, longer, farther. Bigger, stronger, faster.

Last game of season #1. No playoffs. No championship. No glory. Only an opportunity.

"One last thing. From the depths of ineptitude 5 weeks ago to this..."

Everyone looked to the scoreboard.

Niagara X-Men   36
Buffalo State College   38

00:00
4th quarter

"Keep playing. Play until you can't play no more. Go to university. Get an education. Life is a gift. Do something with it. Don't waste it. Make an impact in this world. Create a legacy. And, don't be lazy. Get in the weight room. Tonight!"

At some point during this final game, Season 2 started.

Ohhhh, Caaaanada.

Epilogue

The referee walked past our post-game huddle.

"You haven't got a lot of players, coach, but they have a ton of heart."

No smug look. No *"Eh."*

"Yes, sir. They're good people. Not one asshole."

∞

Endnotes

General Van Riper reference:

A number of online sources explain the Millennium Challenge:

http://www.freerepublic.com/focus/news/745564/posts

http://www.pbs.org/wgbh/nova/wartech/nature.html

However, the most famous reference is in Chapter 4 of *Blink.*

Gladwell, Malcolm (2005). Blink: The power of thinking without thinking. Little, Brown and Company. Time Warner Book Group. New York, N.Y.

∞

Tipping Point reference:

Gladwell, Malcolm (2000). The Tipping Point: How little things can make a big difference. Little, Brown and Company. Time Warner Book Group. New York, N.Y.

Thanks to the Thiel University, Pa., registrar for mailing me this book. I strongly recommend this outstanding bestseller.

∞

Guerilla Ontology reference:

Guerilla Ontology is a concept developed by legendary author Robert Anton Wilson. *Lost and Philosophy* provided an interpretation.

Robert Anton Wilson, The Illuminatus Trilogy, http://rawilson. com/illuminatus.html

Lost and Philosophy (2008) edited by Sharon M. Kaye. Blackwell Publishing. Pages 106-8, chapter 9 Lost, The Third Policeman, and Guerilla Ontology by Jessica Engelking.

∞

Cognitive Dissonance reference:

Leon Festinger is a prominent social psychologist who developed a theory which suggests that inconsistency between beliefs and conduct causes psychological tension and discomfort, an internal stress that motivates a person to change — change beliefs to fit actions or change actions to fit behaviour.

Festinger, L. (1957). A theory of cognitive dissonance. Evanston, IL: Row, Peterson.

∞

Acedia reference:

Acedia is one of the "Seven Deadly Sins" linked to the works of the 4th century Monk, Evagrius Ponticus. St. Thomas Aquinas interpreted acedia in Summa Theologiae. Lost and Philosophy provided a modern interpretation of St. Thomas Aquinas' work.

Aquinas, Thomas & Heath, Thomas R. (2006). Summa Theologiae, Consequences of Charity. Cambridge University Press.

Lost and Philosophy (2008) edited by Sharon M. Kaye. Blackwell Publishing pp. 245-6, chapter 20 Aquinas and Rose on Faith and Reason by Daniel B. Gallagher.

∞

Enjoy the book?
We would like to hear from you.

Post a review on Amazon, Goodreads or let us know directly at
reviews@ginoarcaro.com.

Follow Gino on Social Media

GinoArcaro

@Gino_Arcaro

+GinoArcaro

GinoArcaro

Gino's Blog

Follow Jordan Publications Inc. on Social Media
for up-to-the-minute information on Gino and his books

GinoArcaro.Author

@JordanPubInc

+GinoArcaroBooks

More Books by Gino Arcaro

Soul of a Lifter

Gino Arcaro's journey from childhood obesity to natural health and strength was not made alone; he relied on the Soul of a Lifter. In telling this tale, Arcaro draws on life lessons learned from his careers as a football coach, police officer and college teacher to inspire and lead the reader in a soul-searching quest to reach his/her own potential. This is not your run-of-the-mill motivational book. Discover insights about what drives the soul... what happens when you listen and when you don't!

Selling H.E.L.L. in Hell
from the series Soul of an Entrepreneur

You may be starting out in business or just contemplating making the big decision. Gino Arcaro knows what you're thinking and wants to make sure you know what you're not thinking. His thought-bending tales, while entertaining and steeped in reality, will make the would-be business owner take a second and third look at the situation before jumping in. And, for those already "self-employed," Arcaro offers a unique slant on dealing with day-to-day customer and employee challenges.

eXplode: X Fitness Training System

Sought after his entire adult life to help others achieve their workout goals, Arcaro put his weight lifting theories and routines into this manual. His "Case Studies," true stories from his 40+ years of working out (completely natural) bring a sense of reality to the average gym-goer who just wants to get in shape, stay in shape, and most-importantly, not quit. No gimmicks, just discussion and formulas that can be tailored to any situation regardless of how long or how intensely one has been working out.

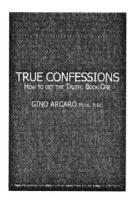

True Confessions

Gino Arcaro relates and upholds a simple fact: "Everyone has a conscience. No exceptions. If you're alive, you have a conscience. The myth of 'no conscience' actually means 'weak or dysfunctional' conscience." Therefore, a truth-seeker must appeal to the conscience, meaning, "make the conscience work out, make it work right, and make it do all the work." True Confessions is a manual for anyone whose job it is to get the truth. For example, Human Resources personnel during the job interview process or Law Enforcement interviewers who can use Arcaro's theories to open a window into the psyche of a suspect under interrogation.

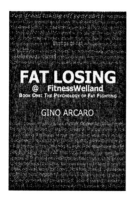

Fat Losing: The psychology of fat fighting

"Waste Mis-management leads to Waist Mis-management"

This is not a diet book. This 40-page eBook explains the most important truth about fighting fat: it begins at the top – literally. Without a proper mindset, no amount of dieting or counting calories will workout. Digesting Fat Losing is the first step to understanding how to change your habits and thinking for once and for all. It contains practical discussions that engage the reader in re-thinking the obstacles that stand in the way of becoming a healthier person. Gino Arcaro, a self-proclaimed "dysfunctional 12-year-old, trying to overcome my obesity," is an expert on the subject. He's written Fat Losing to share what he has learned and practiced for over 40 years.

Be Fit Don't Quit

Full of exercise ideas young children can try on their own or with a parent, this book will rekindle in any adult a love for the simple act of playing. Gino Arcaro has spent his life working out and teaching young adults about the importance of "being fit." He wrote Be Fit Don't Quit to express a tried-and-true message: Exercising is natural and fun. Never quit!

SWAT Offense

By connecting partial concepts that can build any formation, any pass play and any running play to fit the situation, at the line of scrimmage, Arcaro has designed a system that eliminates the need for a conventional playbook that has to be memorized. Memorization is replaced by translation of a simple language. He designed the SWAT offense as a solution to a nightmarish reality of limitations – poor talent and poor resources, a one-man coaching staff, open-admission players, and on top of it all, out-matched opponents…willingly sought out! David constantly calling out Goliath. Arcaro's SWAT offense is the most unique offensive system you'll ever see because it has limitless offense capacity but no playbook. A unique feature of the SWAT Offense is its ties to SWAT Defense.

SWAT Defense

Making the defensive call has never been harder. Coordinators have the greatest challenges in football history. Spread no-huddle offenses, extreme passing, clock-changing rules. More to defend, less time to think. Arcaro's SWAT Defense shows how to beat the spread by forcing the offense to go deep and crack under pressure. "A stress-filled workplace for quarterbacks and receivers leads to an explosion." Central to Arcaro's system is his decision-making model that teaches defensive coordinators and players to make the right calls – those split-second decisions that have to be made about 60 times per game. Making the right call is not easy. Like any skill, defensive decision-makers need guidelines and experience to develop into full potential. A unique feature of the SWAT Defense is its ties to Arcaro's SWAT Offense.

For more free book previews or to purchase Gino's books go to
WWW.GINOARCARO.COM